The Entrepreneurial Thinking of Marcus Crassus

Also, by Robert Lerner

Nonfiction

Entrepreneurship and Ethics in Ancient Rome

Customer Acquisition Strategies

Career Turbulence

Fiction

An Accidental Prophet

The Cinderella Vessel

Dog Park Diaries

The Entrepreneurial Thinking of Marcus Crassus

By

Robert Lerner

Front Cover Photo courtesy of <u>itti ratanakiranaworn</u> and Shutterstock.com
Back Cover Photo courtesy of Diagram Lajard

Author's note on citations and sources: The primary ancient biographical source on Crassus' life is Plutarch's Lives *(an 1892 translation by G. Long is available at Project Gutenberg,* http://www.gutenberg.org/*). All direct quotations from Plutarch are from Long's translation, and they are immediately followed by the source citation of book name and section (for example, Plutarch, Crassus 4; Plutarch, Sulla 7). Other quotes, images, tables, or sentences requiring a reference are directly followed in the text by a citation with author, date, and page (with a full source reference available in the notes and bibliography), photographer and source, or other relevant identifying information. Robber baron or other quotes are from* brainyquote.com*, unless shown otherwise. Images used in this text without attribution are in the public domain.*

Table of Contents

Acknowledgements

In this book, I examine an ancient Roman aristocrat's business methods. I hoped to learn that my subject was unduly criticized for his approaches to wealth creation and perhaps partially rehabilitate his legacy. Unfortunately, as my examination of the man progressed, I discovered far too little good and much more bad and ugly than I expected. Fortunately, much can still be learned from the bad and the ugly as well as the good, and I have had the good fortune of having many friends help me in the task.

I owe a great debt to Dr. Jacqueline Carlon. This book would not have been possible without her review and commentary. And I am grateful to Susan Andres for her meticulous editing of this text. I would also like to thank Mark Kozak-Holland, Dr. Glen Wegner, Ehsan Moghimi, Jerry Kappus, Shelli Mehri, Dan Butler, and Nathalie Villeneuve for their extensive feedback on the book's early drafts, of which there were many. Any errors, omissions, or misinterpretation of source material are solely my responsibility.

Last, I thank my wonderful wife for her uncomplaining toleration of the years I spent devoted to Marcus Crassus and the robber barons of the Gilded Age.

Introduction

Crassus: Of Myth and Man

Possibly many Romans of Marcus Licinius Crassus' generation (he was born circa 115 BC) did not know of the myth that young Crassus was forced to survive eight months in a cave of a Spanish landowner who provided him with food and the services of two beautiful slave girls. But likely most knew he was the Roman Republic's wealthiest politician, the man whose legions defeated Spartacus, and also that he lost his life in an unnecessary battle with the Parthian Empire (now part of modern Iran and Turkey).

Figure I.1. A marble bust assumed to be Crassus because it was found in one of his descendants' tombs.

But Crassus' life story did not end in his humiliating military defeat and death, for the victorious Parthians, to mock Crassus' unquenchable thirst for wealth, desecrated his corpse by pouring "molten gold into his mouth" (Dio, *Roman History* 40.27.3).

Historians and Crassus

Unfortunately, but perhaps deservedly so, ancient and modern historians have treated Crassus' life and his business interests nearly as brutally as the Parthians treated his corpse. What the Parthians supposedly did with gold (figure 1.2), historians achieved with their ink—the eternal blackening of Crassus' legacy.

Figure I.2. The infamous death of the greedy Crassus as reported by the ancient writer Cassius Dio and retold in a 1560 edition of *Pegme,* an illustrated French text by Pierre Coustau.

For nearly two thousand years, Crassus has been denounced for his repeatedly demonstrated lust for money and for his humiliating military defeat at the hands of a smaller Parthian army. However, in the historians' defense, Crassus made himself an easy target.

Adding to Crassus' modern infamy is that his greatest military victory was over the gladiator Spartacus and his army of rebelling slaves seeking freedom from their Roman oppressors (figure I.3). In the last half-century, Spartacus has enjoyed a media-generated resurgence of interest—a TV series inspired by his life on STARZ and a video game based on his bloody exploits—all at the expense of Marcus Crassus.

Figure I.3. An 1882 image of Spartacus' courageous death in 71 BC at the hands of Crassus' legions.

But perhaps the greatest modern indignity for Crassus' reputation is that the name Spartacus, based on the 1960 movie of the same name starring Kirk Douglas, still reverberates in popular culture as a cry of freedom. In the movie, after his defeat by Crassus, each of Spartacus' surviving soldiers seeks to protect their defeated leader's identification by crying, "I'm Spartacus." Crassus, played by Sir Laurence Olivier, proceeds to crucify all the defeated slaves—as did the historical Crassus, for crucifixion was standard punishment for rebellious slaves. Thus, the result is the same whether Crassus' depiction is drawn from Hollywood or the historical record—the name Crassus, unlike that of Spartacus, today languishes in villainy and ignominy.

Buried beneath the multitude of myths associated with the man's extraordinary life and gruesome death hides Crassus' entrepreneurial genius. For the enigmatic Crassus repeatedly showed himself as a financial wizard who, through his shrewd investments, reached the pinnacle of power in the Late Roman Republic. Unfortunately, a result of all his machinations (which possibly included bankrolling Julius Caesar's early career) was that he also contributed significantly to the demise of the very political system in which he prospered.

The Greek-born historian Plutarch (c. AD 50–AD 120) wrote our sole surviving ancient biography of Crassus approximately 150 years after Crassus' death (Grant 1970, 310).[1] Yet, he still set the foundation on which rests modern history's judgment of Crassus' life, accomplishments, and his sins. Despite his apparent distaste for Crassus, Plutarch (figure I.4) acknowledged the importance of Crassus' victory over Spartacus to his fellow aristocratic slave owners and also the effect of Crassus' defeat by the Parthians on the stability of the Late Roman Republic.

Figure I.4. An imagined image of Plutarch from a 1565 French translation of Parallel Lives, Plutarch's biographical work containing a history of Crassus' life.

Crassus' stunning defeat also became a cause for derision not only because a much smaller adversary destroyed his legions and he forfeited his life, but more important for the Romans, Crassus lost his legions' military standards—honored symbols of the senate and people of Rome. Thus, Crassus, became the fodder for criticism by generations of historians, beginning with Plutarch.

Unfortunately, Plutarch, in telling the story of Crassus' life and death, offers only glimpses of the moneymaking activities central to his behavior, and does so to reinforce negative character traits of Crassus whose business practices at times exceeded the limits of acceptability. Senators risked removal from the Senate if their commercial activities strayed too far afield from property-based sources of income—mines, agricultural production, and real estate (buying, selling, renting). Lending money to friends was also acceptable, even expected, and most senators set up their freed slaves in other businesses to share in their profits. However, many played fast and loose with the rules, and likely Crassus was among the worst offenders.

A Contemporary's Views of Crassus

Besides Plutarch's biography, we have contemporary comments on Crassus from Marcus Cicero (Figure I.5) who was often politically opposed to Crassus. Cicero was so famous an orator and popular author in his day that many of his letters and books have survived. Cicero rose to political power on the strength of his intellect and on merit, rather than on his family's history, wealth, or military glory.

Despite Cicero's self-made achievements, he articulated most upper-class Romans' opinion in his book *On Duties* (150) where he declared business inappropriate for a gentleman. He then went on to describe businessmen as vulgar. This condemnation of businessmen came despite Cicero and his fellow Roman senators'

Figure I.5. A bust of Cicero (in Madrid's Prado Gallery), a contemporary of Crassus and a key source of information on Crassus' character.

willingness to avail themselves of the business services Crassus offered his fellow senators, such as readily available credit, talented slaves for hire, and prime real estate for purchase. It should be noted that Cicero's most biting criticism of Crassus came only *after* his death at the Parthians' hands, but from his colorful commentary much insight into Crassus' character can be drawn (as did Plutarch).

Modern Historians on Crassus and His Legacy

Like Plutarch, modern historians tend to focus on Crassus' generation of wealth as an end (that is, greed) or as a means to obtain political power from which to derive further wealth. Professor Allen Ward, who diverges from most historians with his objective biography of Crassus, opens his book *Marcus Crassus and the Late Roman Republic* (1977) with a summary of seven modern scholars' characterizations of Crassus.[2] Phrases and words those historians used to describe Crassus include love of money, adept in the tricks of Roman finance, calculating bourgeois, crafty, speculator, and hard-headed man of business.

Conversely, in a detailed review of the modern literature describing the successful "entrepreneurial personality" (Mintzberg, Ahlstrand & Lampel 2005, 123–147), we find the following qualities delineated: tough, pragmatic, independent, controlling, risk taker, obsessive, calculating, crafty, attuned to environmental changes, defensive, revolutionary, opportunistic, biased, bold, inspirational, unwilling to submit to authority, and conformity-averse.[3] We now admire much of what the ancient Roman and modern historians condemn in Crassus the businessman! Historians also routinely criticize Crassus for his lack of political constancy "to any cause except his own" (Holland 2003, 136).[4] As part of this condemnation, historians also view Crassus' relationship and power-sharing alliance with Julius Caesar (figure I.6) as tantamount to helping in the Roman Republic's suicide.

Figure I.6. Bust Julius Caesar in the National Archaeological Museum of Naples (Photo by Andreas Wahra).

As we examine Crassus the businessperson, we have many hurdles to overcome.

Why Study Crassus?

In my first book, *Entrepreneurship and Ethics in Ancient Rome: The Management Lessons of Pliny the Younger*, I used elements of Crassus' life and wealth acquisition techniques as counterexamples to Pliny the Younger's ethical behavior (Lerner 2013).[5] However, as lurid and effective as the examples presented were for that comparison, I thought perhaps I continued the negative stereotyping of Crassus, and I was determined to analyze Crassus' life and business activities at some point.

Crassus accrued great wealth in turbulent times and leveraged that wealth to obtain political power (Lerner 2014);[6] unfortunately, ancient writers left us little. Even Crassus' bust, shown in figure I.1, is attributed to Crassus without certainty (as opposed to the busts of Cicero and Caesar shown in figures I.5 and I.6). As for modern scholarship, the three essential English language biographies of Crassus were all written more than forty years ago. Two books were written in the 1970s: (1) the book by Allen Ward (1977) previously referenced and (2) *Marcus Crassus: A Political Biography* written by B. A. Marshall (1976).[7] The third biography, *Marcus Crassus Millionaire* by Sir Frank Adcock was published in 1966 and spans fewer than sixty-five pages.[8] If you enter "Marcus Crassus" as a book search on Amazon™, there are fewer than 100 "hits."

Enter "Julius Caesar," and there are more than 7,000; for "Cicero," more than 10,000. Crassus' life has not been blessed with anywhere near the academic interest his ancient peers have received.

The Original Goal of This Text

As I re-examined Plutarch and Cicero for insight into Crassus' business dealings, I intended to rehabilitate my original opinions of the man and his character. Unfortunately, the more I studied the sources and commentary, I concluded that the accepted consensus (both ancient and modern) is accurate. There is little to admire in the man's character, and Crassus truly obsessed over gaining great wealth. When Crassus died, his fortune amounted to more than 7,100 talents of gold (Plutarch, *Crassus* 2). With a talent approximately equal to 71 pounds, this amounts to more than 500,000 pounds of gold. Today, with gold at about $1,650 an ounce, that wealth would have amounted to a fortune of over $13 billion, as shown in table I.1.

However, I also examined how Crassus accumulated his vast wealth, and was surprised to find, despite his significant ethical lapses, that there was much to respect in his ability to innovate. I saw a strong link between some business methods (good, bad and ugly) of this ancient businessperson and the greatest entrepreneurs of America's Gilded Age—the men known today as the *robber barons.*

Table I.1. Approximate Conversion Rates of an Ancient Talent of Gold to US Dollars Today.

Gold	Dollars (Today)
1 ounce (1 oz.)	$1,650
1 pound (16 oz.)	$26,400
1 talent (71 lbs.)	$1,874,400
7,100 talents	$13,308,200,000

Was Crassus the Original Robber Baron?

In the late nineteenth century, the term *robber baron* came into use to describe businesspersons who made great fortunes through aggressive, exploitive, ruthless, and illegal business practices. The questionable practices of the robber barons included the following transgressions:

- Using political influence for personal financial gain
- Bribery
- Monopolistic control of resources such as oil and steel
- Stock manipulation

- Paying low wages

- Breaking labor strikes through violence

- Using predatory pricing or secret, preferential rebates to gain a monopoly

- Raising prices exorbitantly once a market was cornered.

Figure I.7. In this Samuel Ehrhardt cartoon, America's robber barons collect tribute from the people and their elected officials. (Puck, c. 1889, courtesy Special Collections and Archives, Georgia State University.)

This text references three robber barons with some of their major business interests and sins: J. P. Morgan (figure I.8), John D. Rockefeller (figure I.9), and Cornelius Vanderbilt (figure I.10).

Figure I.8. J. P. Morgan (1837–1913) helped form US Steel (from the merger of the Carnegie Steel Company, the Federal Steel Company, and the Consolidated Steel and Wiring Company) and General Electric (from the merger of Edison General Electric and Thompson-Houston Electric Company). Banking clients included the Astors, Guggenheims, DuPonts, and Vanderbilts (Chernow 2010, xii).[9] In 1896, Morgan financed Adolph Simon Och's purchase of the New York Times. Morgan also helped the US government end the Panic of 1893 and the Panic of 1907. Today, JPMorgan Chase & Company (2019) has assets of $2.7 trillion.[10]

Figure I.9. John D. Rockefeller (1839–1937) cofounded and ran Standard Oil from 1870 to 1897, consolidating and controlling America's oil business. In the process, Rockefeller likely became the richest person in world history with an estimated wealth today calculated at $192 billion. In 1911, the US government broke Standard Oil into several companies that today include ExxonMobil, Conoco, Chevron, Pennzoil, and Amoco (*New York Times* 2007).[11]

Figure I.10. Cornelius Vanderbilt's (1794–1877) rise began when he was an aggressive steamboat entrepreneur whose assets included the Staten Island Ferry. Vanderbilt invested in railroads during the Civil War, and his wealth today is estimated at $142 billion (*New York Times* 2007).[12]

Perhaps the best description of the robber barons can be generalized from the T. J. Stiles description of Cornelius Vanderbilt in his Pulitzer Prize-winning book, *The First Tycoon: The Epic Life* of *Cornelius Vanderbilt*. Stiles (2010, 116) says of Vanderbilt that he was "an instinctive predator, and, like every predator, he was drawn to the scent of the sick and the vulnerable."[13]

We see, as this text progresses, that many predatory traits of the robber barons of the nineteenth century can be discerned in Crassus' actions. To buttress this assertion, as we move through the text, comments by and about the robber barons are used to highlight their close resemblance to the ancient world's much-criticized business tycoon, Marcus Crassus.

The ancient/modern resemblance does not stop at exploitation or a willingness to bend their social standards, for we also see in Crassus, much like the robber barons of the Gilded Age, brilliant flashes of entrepreneurial thinking. For our purposes, *entrepreneurial thinking* means the innovative thought process needed for achieving business success that requires the following attributes in the entrepreneur: vision, flexibility, confidence, tenacity, opportunism, and passion (Mintzberg, Ahlstrand & Lampel 2005, 123–147). These attributes are described in table I.2.

If Crassus and the robber barons shared any positive characteristics, it was their ability innovate on a grand scale and to conceive significant profit opportunities. Unfortunately, it was often in the single-minded pursuit of profit from those ideas that these businessmen displayed their most insidious ethical and moral lapses.

	Attribute	Description
1	Vision	Possessing the ability to identify and capitalize on opportunities in the marketplace (for example, a new or improved product, service, or method)
2	Flexibility	Possessing the ability to recalibrate or fine-tune your vision's implementation based on new information or experiences
3	Confidence	Possessing the courage to ignore past failures and overcome current constraints to make the difficult decisions required to carry out your vision
4	Tenacity	Possessing the determination and perseverance to achieve the successful implementation of your vision
5	Opportunism	Possessing an outlook that facilitates the exploitation of circumstances in the marketplace for the benefit of your business
6	Passion	Possessing the desire to pursue your vision despite the challenges and risks

Timeline of Major Events

Date (BC)	Major Event	Age of Crassus
c. 115	Birth of Marcus Licinius Crassus (Crassus)	Born
106	Birth of Marcus Tullius Cicero (Cicero)	9
106	Birth of Gnaeus Pompeius Magnus (Pompey the Great)	9
100	Birth of Gaius Julius Caesar (Caesar)	15
c. 97/96–93	Crassus with his father in Spain	18/19–22
88	Start of Sullan civil war	27
87–84	Lucius Cornelius Cinna (Cinna) serves as consul of Rome	
87	Suicide of Crassus' father	28
85	Crassus' departure for Spain	30

84	Death of Cinna	31
84	Crassus recruits his force of 2,500 soldiers	31
83	Crassus joins with Sulla	32
82	Lucius Cornelius Sulla Felix (Sulla) victorious and named dictator	33
82/81	Sulla proscribes political opponents	33/34
81	Sulla expands the Roman Senate from 300 to 600 and enrolls Crassus in the Roman Senate	34
81/80	Pompey awarded his first triumph	34/35
79	Cicero defends Sextus Roscius Amerinus	36
78	Sulla's death	36
73	Trial of Crassus and Licinia, a vestal virgin	42
73	The Rebellion of Spartacus begins	42
72	Crassus commands Roman forces against Spartacus	43

71	Crassus defeats Spartacus	44
71	Pompey awarded his second triumph	44
70	Crassus and Pompey serve as consuls of Rome	45
70	Crassus dedicates 10 percent of his wealth to Hercules	45
63	Cicero serves as consul of Rome	52
63	Caesar becomes pontifex maximus (chief priest)	52
63	Birth of Gaius Octavius (future Emperor Augustus)	54
61	Pompey awarded his third triumph	54
60	Crassus, Pompey, and Caesar form First Triumvirate	55
59	Caesar serves as consul of Rome	56
58	Cicero exiled	57
58	Caesar begins the Gallic Wars	57
57	Cicero returns from exile	58

55	Crassus and Pompey serve as consuls of Rome	60
55 & 54	Caesar invades Britain	60
54	Crassus given control of the province of Syria	61
53	Crassus defeated and killed in Parthia	61
49	Start of Caesar's Civil War	

Description of Key Historical Figures in this Book

Name (DOB–DOD)	Description
Atticus (109 BC–32 BC)	Wealthy Roman financier and lifelong friend of and correspondent with Cicero
Caesar (100 BC–44 BC)	Consul in 59 BC; debtor to Crassus; triumvir with Crassus and Pompey; dictator of Rome 48 BC–44 BC; assassinated on March 15, 44 BC
Cicero (106 BC–43 BC)	Consul in 63 BC; exiled in 58 BC; returned to Rome in 57 BC; lawyer, orator, politician, author, correspondent with Atticus
Cinna (Died 84 BC)	Consul 87 BC–84 BC, ordered the death of Crassus' father and older brother in 87 BC, murdered by his soldiers in 84 BC
Hercules	Son of the god Jupiter and a mortal mother, to whom victorious Roman generals donated 10 percent of their booty

Licinia	Vestal virgin accused of criminal intercourse with Crassus in 73 BC
P. Licinius Crassus (Died 87 BC)	Crassus' father, consul in 97 BC, governor of Further Spain 96–93 BC, committed suicide in 87 BC rather than yield to a victorious Cinna
Pompey (106 BC–48 BC)	Roman general, consul with Crassus in 70 BC and 55 BC, sole consul in 52 BC, triumvir with Crassus and Caesar
Spartacus (c. 111 BC–71 BC)	An escaped gladiator who fielded more than seventy thousand slaves in a rebellion against the Roman Republic; defeated by Crassus in 71 BC
Sulla (c. 138 BC–78 BC)	Consul in 88 BC and 82 BC, dictator from 82–81 BC, Crassus' commanding officer during the civil war
Tertulla	Widow of Crassus' older brother, wife of Crassus, and mother of Crassus' two sons (Publius and Marcus)

Definition of Robber Baron

Robber Baron (Oxforddictionaries.com)

Noun. An unscrupulous plutocrat, especially an American capitalist who acquired a fortune in the late nineteenth century by ruthless means.

Origin

Originally denoting a feudal lord who engaged in plundering.

Chapter 1. **War and Opportunity**

Background on the Roman Republic

The Roman Republic had already survived for more than 400 years before Crassus' birth. Romans believed the city of Rome was founded in 753 BC and ruled by kings until 509 BC, when a revolt incited by a handful of aristocrats overthrew their tyrannical sovereign and established the Roman Republic. Over the next four centuries, the small city-state of Rome grew into an empire that spanned east to west from what is now western Asia to Spain and north to south from France to North Africa (figure 1.1).

In the Roman Republic, to deter any one man's royal aspirations, the male citizens elected two senators as consuls with "king-like" authority for one year (but re-election occurred on rare occasions). In the Late Republic, the period of Crassus' life, restrictions on consuls' terms were relaxed (or demanded by powerful generals), which contributed greatly to the Republic's fall, as individual men could attain greater power for longer and longer durations.

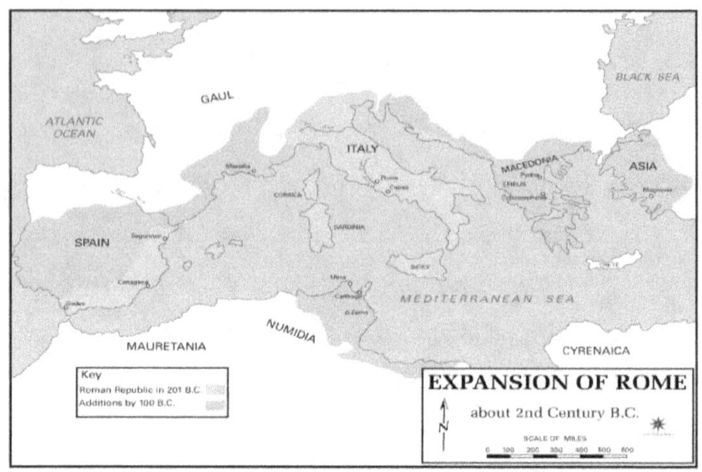

Figure 1.1. The extent of the Roman Republic at the
time of Crassus' birth.

Figure 1.2. A 19thcentury fresco by Cesare Maccari depicts the
Roman Senate in 63 BC. A shunned senator, Lucius Sergius Catilina
(Catiline) is accused of conspiring to overthrow the Republic.
(See appendix A.)

Power in the Late Republic

Rome expanded in the second century BC, and by Crassus' birth, great wealth and power was consolidated in the hands of a small cadre of powerful senatorial families. This increase in wealth directly resulted from conquests in the second century BC. Individual power accumulated, not just from the influx of wealth, but also from creating a professional army, whose allegiance was usually to its commanding general. That wealth and power also made many senators far less inclined to work with their peers to solve the problems of the day than they had in the past. This period also saw the rise of factions to counter the more powerful senators' influence. The result of mixing money, power, and factionalism was paralysis—the government didn't act cohesively on significant problems emerging from the Republic's rapid expansion.

The Republic teetered on a dangerous precipice as politicians further compounded their problems by leveraging sensitive political issues (for example, land redistribution to the poor and grain pricing) to incite mob violence and gain more power. The senators' willingness to also use the law courts to humiliate an opponent and burnish their public personae added to the period's volatility. The mob was often swayed as much by a senator's performance in the courts as by the verdicts rendered. Because of these stresses, as shown in figure 1.3, fissures formed in the fabric of Rome's senate-led government, and the Republic lurched from crises to crises while debate devolved into physical violence and civil war.

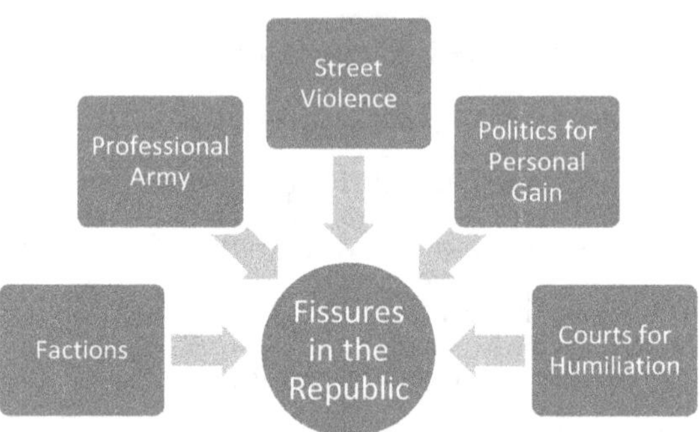

Figure 1.3. The stresses that tore the Roman Republic's fabric of government in the first century BC.

Four periods of civil war were associated with the Roman Republic's collapse and Imperial Rome's emergence under the rule of one leader—the Emperor. The first period of the civil wars (Sulla's Civil War—88 BC–80 BC) and the events leading to the second period of civil war (Caesar's Civil War—49 BC–45 BC) are this text's focus (see Timeline of Major Events). This text does not cover the third civil war fought following Caesar's assassination (the Liberator's Civil War—43 BC–42 BC) and the fourth civil war (the Final War of the Roman Republic—32 BC–30 BC). The fourth civil war was fought between Mark Antony (with Cleopatra) and Caesar's grandnephew Octavian, who became Rome's first emperor, Caesar Augustus.

Civil War and Crassus

The Sullan civil war first erupted when Crassus was in his twenties and resulted in his father's suicide and in the death of Crassus' surviving older brother. His father took his life rather than surrender to his enemies. Lucius Cornelius Cinna, four-time consul (87 BC–84 BC) and father-in-law of Julius Caesar, controlled the winning side in Rome during this period. Crassus was not executed with his brother because he was likely thought too unimportant. After the death of his father and brother, Crassus inherited the family's assets. Plutarch reported that the family's wealth at the time was *only* 300 talents—over half a billion dollars today!

As time passed, opposition to Cinna gathered strength and coalesced around Cornelius Sulla (figure 1.4), a former consul in 88 BC and a general who fought a war in the Republic's easternmost sphere of interest (modern Turkey). By 85 BC, Cinna viewed any potential Sullan sympathizers in Rome as dangerous enemies, and their lives were at risk. This threat, according to Plutarch (*Crassus*, 4), forced Crassus' departure from Rome.

Figure 1.4. Bust of Sulla in the Naples Archeological Museum
(photo by Robert Lerner).

Crassus made his way to Hispania Ulterior (the southern part
of modern Spain, figure 1.5), where his father was once governor
and family assets likely remained. Crassus left his wife Tertulla and
a child behind and, with a small retinue of three friends and ten
slaves, made his way to the Iberian coast where he remained in
hiding for eight months (Plutarch, *Crassus* 4).

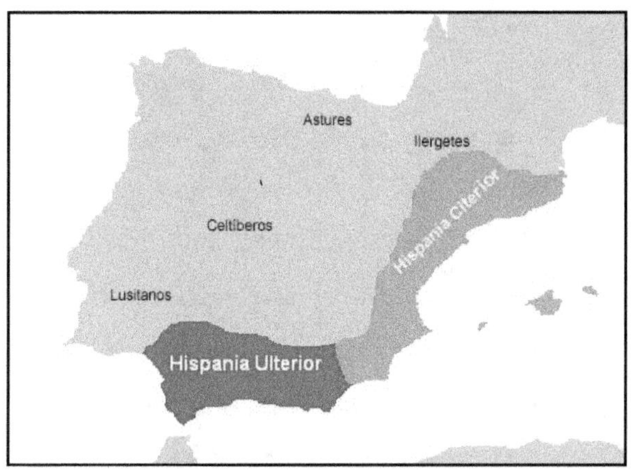

Figure 1.5. Hispania Ulterior (Further Spain) and Hispania Citerior (Nearer Spain) as of 197 BC.

From here, we must let Plutarch tell the story of Crassus' exile (*Crassus*, 4):

> *He (Crassus) did not venture to make himself known, but sought refuge in a tract bordering on the sea, belonging to Vibius Pacianus, where he hid himself in a large cave. He sent a slave to Vibius to sound his disposition; for the provisions that Crassus brought with him were now exhausted. On hearing the news, Vibius was pleased that Crassus had escaped . . . (and) determined to show Crassus every kind of friendly attention; and it occurred to him to*

consider the youth of Crassus, that he was a very young man, and that provision should be made in some degree also for the pleasures suitable to his age, and that merely to supply his wants would argue that he was serving Crassus as little as he could, rather than with hearty zeal; accordingly, he took with him two handsome female slaves, and went down to the seacoast. When he came to the place, he pointed to the road that led up to it, and told them to go in boldly. Crassus, seeing them approach, was afraid that the spot was known, and had been discovered; and, accordingly, he asked them what they wanted, and who they were. The women replied, as they had been instructed, that they were looking for their master, who was concealed there; on which Crassus perceived the joke which Vibius was playing off upon him, and his kind attentions, and received the women; and they stayed with him for the rest of the time, telling and reporting to Vibius what he requested them.

Thus began the survival myth of a youthful, though well-comforted, Crassus. Plutarch, perhaps for validation or just for plain titillation, informed his readers that another Roman writer, who had lived at least until AD 19, even interviewed one of the aged slave girls himself. Plutarch makes much of Crassus' "suffering" for eight months in a cave (with his three friends, ten slaves that traveled with him, and the two female slaves). However, his family's assets in Spain possibly included both tin and silver mines (Plutarch, *Crassus* 2; Ward 1977, 74).[1] Crassus, during this exile, was likely neither alone nor destitute.

Crassus' Exile Ends

While still in exile, Crassus learned that Cinna, who wielded nearly monarchial power, was killed by a mutiny of his army (84 BC). Sulla, who had settled his war in the east, prepared to march against his (and Crassus') remaining enemies who still controlled power in Rome. Crassus determined to raise an armed force of 2,500 men privately (as he was not authorized by anyone in power to do so) and fight beside Sulla. Crassus had the patience to await Cinna's death and Sulla's return; to react any sooner would likely have courted defeat and death. However, once Cinna passed from the scene, Crassus acted decisively and in a fashion that helped slake his desire for vengeance and accumulate immense wealth.

Crassus' Vision of the Future

Crassus' waiting until the opportunity was ripe and expeditiously acting comprise our first example of his entrepreneurial thinking (albeit in the military, not business space). Crassus might have already envisioned raising his army to strike back at his enemies by the time he arrived in Spain. Despite the myth of his eight months in a cave, he must have begun recruiting his soldiers and military staff shortly after his arrival in Spain. We can assume this early planning because Crassus raised *and* transported a 2,500-man army from Spain to the Sullan side within *months* of Cinna's death. The army Crassus created was likely composed of veterans who served under his father when he was governor of Hispania Ulterior, and this would have sped the formation of his military force.

Crassus and an Initial Allegation of Plunder

Plutarch reported that in making his military preparations to join Sulla, young Crassus "plundered" the Spanish port town of Malaca (modern Malaga on Spain's southern coast). Plutarch (*Crassus* 4) also says Crassus always denied the charge and personally "contradicted those that affirmed it." The charge was clearly current in Crassus' lifetime, and he felt the need to refute it.

Even if the Malacans were not plundered, they might have suffered from Crassus' impatience with any reluctance they had to provide or provision the ships he demanded. As Crassus acted on his own authority, the town might have been hard pressed to discern the difference between being plundered and the forced provisioning of an army of 2,500. The port town's shipping capacity would also have been crucial to Crassus, as he looked to sail from the Spanish coast to Africa to meet forces loyal to Sulla. Sailing had the advantage of offering both the speed and the safety a land journey through hostile territory could not.

Crassus Stops in Africa

Crassus departed Spain for Africa trying to join another more senior Sullan supporter, Metellus Pius, a relative of Sulla's wife (Keaveney 2005, 109).[2] Plutarch reports that Crassus had "dissension" with Metellus, but gives no insight into the reason for the quarrel. However, it might have been a disagreement over Crassus' role or perhaps the control of his forces (Ward 1977, 61).[3] Despite the underlying cause or causes, Crassus refused to linger or compromise his plans and sailed with his army to Sulla who was in Greece preparing for his march on Rome.

Crassus Aggressively Pursues His Vision

Crucial elements involved in Crassus' pursuit of revenge can be deduced from the negative information (the "plunder" of the

Malacans and "dissension" with Metellus Pius) Plutarch provided on Crassus' levy of troops and his journey to Sulla. One senses from Plutarch's depiction of events that, once Crassus acted, he was determined to achieve his goals and intolerant of any delay or obstacle in his way. Crassus' unwavering commitment to follow through on his plans provides our first lesson in entrepreneurial thinking.

Lesson 1. Envisage Your Future

Crassus might not have known *when* he could embark on his course of revenge, but he likely had long contemplated *what* that course entailed. So, when the opportunity arose (Cinna's death), Crassus quickly mobilized in pursuit of his remaining enemies. Crassus raised his army and allowed no one to stand between him and carrying out his plan to join Sulla on his march to Rome. Even when Crassus' course required modification in Africa, he adjusted his plans and continued to Sulla with his soldiers, never losing sight of his goal or control of his men.

This lesson is not intended as an admonition to develop a detailed plan of action so much as to recognize the importance of planning a vision of what you want to achieve. A *vision* is not as precise as a strategy, nor as nebulous as a creative idea; instead, as defined by the American Marketing Association, it is "a guiding theme that articulates the nature of the business and its intentions for the future."[4] That "guiding theme" will not develop on its own, and because we cannot always know when opportunity will knock at our door (such as Cinna's death in Crassus' case), we must be well prepared for its arrival.

Plan, But Not Too Much

Too much time preparing and planning (that is, paralysis by analysis), however, can lead to missing opportunities, and it is not required for entrepreneurial success. Research on how much time successful entrepreneurs spend planning supports this belief. In a 1994 *Harvard Business Review* article, Amar Bhide, professor of entrepreneurship at the Harvard Business School, studied the amount of planning by successful entrepreneurs (Bhide 1994, 150–161).[5] Bhide, based on interviews with one hundred founders from *Inc.*'s 1989 list of the five hundred fastest-growing private companies in America, reported that entrepreneurial planning was an oxymoron, with 41 percent of the interviewees having no business plan (figure 1.6)!

From Bhide's research, which a 2007 study by Lang et al. in *Venture Capital* corroborated, many successful entrepreneurs are averse to planning, and they often develop comprehensive plans only when forced by existing or potential stakeholders. However, limited planning should never be confused with limited preparation. There must be a balance, as shown in figure 1.7, between planning enough to be successful when an opportunity presents itself and not so much to suffer from inaction engendered by over analysis.

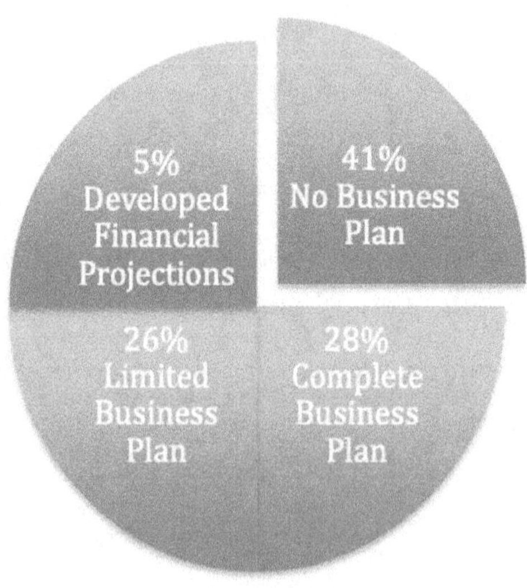

Figure 1.6. Shows the distaste for planning by successful entrepreneurs in 1989 (Bhide 1994, 152)[6] that continues into the twenty-first century (Lange et al. 2007, 237–256).[7]

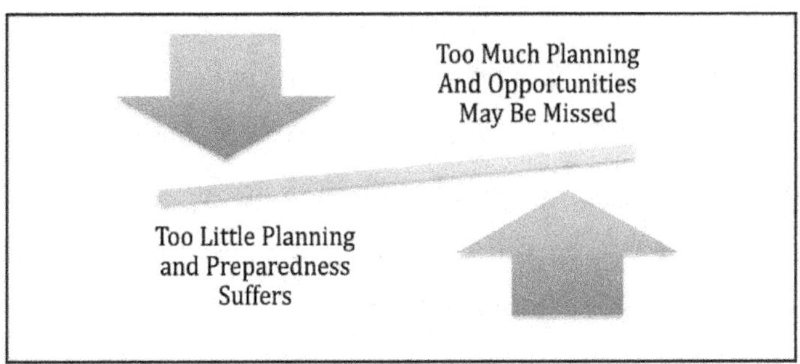

Figure 1.7. Shows the need to find a balance between doing too much planning and missing an opportunity and not doing enough if you intend to be prepared when opportunity knocks.

The word *planner* was absent from Mintzberg's list of successful entrepreneurial personality qualities discussed in this book's introduction. Therefore, although planning is my peculiar passion, I excluded planning as an entrepreneurial thinking attribute in this text, because entrepreneurs and those who study them do not credit detailed planning as a crucial element of their success.

Crassus Raises an Army

Let's spend more time looking at the private army Crassus raised and transported to Sulla. Crassus likely accompanied his father to Spain a decade earlier when the older Crassus was governor (96 BC–93 BC). The younger Crassus probably served in some military capacity for his father, giving him an excellent opportunity to gain military experience when he was in his early twenties (Ward 1977, 49).[8] Crassus would have used that experience and the contacts made during his father's term in office to raise his army and likely drew heavily from the retired legionary veterans in Further Spain. These men would have known his father, if not Crassus himself.

Because Crassus was not even a senator then and lacked any authority to raise an army while in exile, he would have been forced to privately fund his soldiers. Crassus raised a force of 2,500 men, about half a legion at full strength, but legions were rarely near full strength and often under 3,000, so Crassus' achievement was significant.

In his biography of Crassus, Ward (1977, 69, n. 40) estimates that it required about 100 talents to support a legion (soldiers, auxiliaries, cavalry, officers, and so on) for a year. Therefore, Crassus' partial legion would have cost 50 talents (or more than $90 million a year today) to maintain in the field.[9] Crassus likely was forced to borrow some or all required funds (nearly $8 million a month) from creditors (like today's debt financing). The creditors were then repaid from the spoils of victory, and if Crassus were defeated, his creditors counted on sufficient family assets to settle his outstanding debts, even if young Crassus perished in battle.

Crassus Joins Sulla

We can assume Crassus recognized that arriving with 2,500 soldiers provided an opportunity to gain both Sulla's attention and perhaps his gratitude, and Plutarch reports that Sulla welcomed Crassus' support and, perhaps even more, Crassus' troops. When Crassus met Sulla in Greece, the latter had five legions of unknown strength at his command (Ward 1977, 61).[10]

After Sulla and Crassus arrived in Italy, Sulla ordered Crassus to travel the countryside to raise an even larger force. Crassus asked for a military escort, as he was required to pass through enemy territory, but Sulla's warmth was short lived. For Plutarch (*Crassus* 6) tells us that Sulla chastised the youthful Crassus saying, "I give thee as guards thy father, thy brother, thy friends, thy kinsmen, who were cut off illegally and wrongfully, and whose murderers I am now pursuing."

Crassus did not need to be told twice; he left on his mission and completed his duty. As the Sullan forces continued their march to Rome, Crassus must have acquitted himself well, for Sulla, when splitting his army for the final battle of Rome, chose Crassus to lead the right wing (Plutarch, *Crassus* 6).

Crassus and a Second Allegation of Bad Behavior

The important assignment of leading the right wing was made

despite an accusation, detailed by Plutarch (*Crassus* 6), that Crassus sacked the Umbrian town of Tuder (about 90 miles northeast of Rome) but kept most of the booty for himself. Plutarch also indicates that this instance of bad behavior was brought to Sulla's attention. If the story is true, one can hardly imagine legionnaires following such a commander or Sulla giving Crassus such a pivotal assignment in the coming battle.

Another of Sulla's lieutenants helping in the Umbrian campaign was Gnaeus Pompeius (Pompey). Pompey, like Crassus, lost his father (a former consul and commanding general of anti-Cinna forces) during the civil unrest of the period (Seager 2002, 21–23).[11] Pompey, like Crassus, provided an army for Sulla, but his contribution consisted of his father's three legions (Seager 2002, 26), the first of Pompey's many achievements that fueled Crassus' lifetime of jealousy.[12]

Given the future political rivalry between Crassus and Pompey, it is difficult to imagine Pompey not citing the Tuder incident as a concrete example of Crassus' bad behavior. If the event occurred, Pompey should have known it, even if he did not hear of it from Sulla or his aides. If Crassus deprived his soldiers of their booty, they would have been disgruntled, and word of their unhappiness would have reached Pompey's soldiers and Pompey himself. Pompey and his men served in the same theater of operations as

Crassus and his legionnaires. A more likely explanation for the charge of Crassus cheating his troops is that the story is fiction and Plutarch, writing over a century and a half after the events, found some source hostile to the mature Crassus. The tale fit Plutarch's carefully crafted depiction of the influential but avaricious powerbroker the young man was to become, so he used it in Crassus' biography.

Sulla Victorious

Sulla's choice of Crassus to lead his right wing was fortunate. Crassus and his soldiers won a crucial victory in the battle for Rome, which saved a faltering Sulla and helped end the civil war (Plutarch, *Crassus* 6). Sulla was unlikely to forget this debt to Crassus. Plutarch tells us the epitaph Sulla chose for himself was "in substance, that none of his friends ever did him a kindness, and none of his enemies ever did him a wrong, without being fully repaid" (Plutarch, *Sulla* 37). Crassus, with his role in Sulla's victory found himself, at least for the time, in the friends column, but not so highly regarded or feared as Pompey.

Pompey still had the loyalty of his father's three legions serving Sulla (Seager 2002, 26).[13] Sulla rewarded Pompey with the title Magnus (the Great) (Plutarch, *Pompeius* 9.13). Sulla also rewarded the newly titled Pompey the Great with the engagement of his stepdaughter. Sulla's early generosity toward Crassus' future rival for supreme power in Rome likely provoked great jealousy on Crassus' part.

Cicero on Sulla and Crassus

Years later, Cicero, a political ally of Pompey the Great, said of both Sulla and Crassus that the two would "stoop to anything, truckle to anybody, if only they may gain their ends" (*On Duties* I.109). In the period immediately after Sulla's victory, those shared ends entailed making their hated enemies pay with their lives and their fortunes.

Crassus' actions, built on the creation and contribution of his private army, helped Sulla achieve victory, and with that victory, Crassus had his vengeance. His determination to build his success on a foundation of a military force, which he created, tenaciously superintended, and delivered to Sulla, forms our second lesson in entrepreneurial thinking.

Lesson 2. Control Your Future

Crassus, by funding his military force, created greater freedom of action and flexibility for himself than if he ended his exile and joined Sulla as a solitary disaffected noble. Alone, he would have depended on Sulla; with an army, he had leverage. The lesson for the modern entrepreneur to draw from Crassus' actions is to never depend on others for your success. People can and will help you, but if you depend too much on others, especially at crucial junctures in your career or at a time of intense turbulence, you are vulnerable to their failings. And their failure might impede achieving your long-term goals and even your short-term objectives.

This lesson is not to justify what Crassus did militarily. The lesson is to point out that sometimes in business, especially when conflicts arise, the entrepreneur must exercise enough influence and control of his or her stakeholders to allow sufficient freedom of action to facilitate success. Far too often, an entrepreneur's stakeholders (figure 1.8) lose confidence, exclusively focus on their risk exposure, or force an early end to the venture.

Because so many new ventures fail, stakeholders operate rationally, but their nervousness and doubts can prompt the result they look to avoid. Therefore, the entrepreneur must have and maintain enough control and influence to ensure the startup is not prematurely discarded.

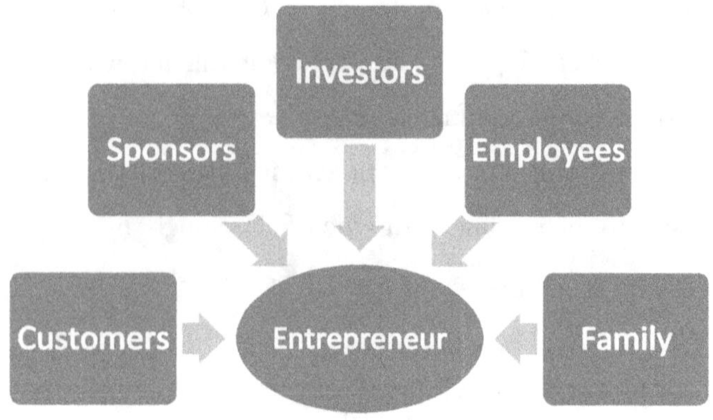

Figure 1.8. Stakeholders with whom the entrepreneur must maintain sufficient autonomy of action and support, or conflicting objectives and different risk sensitivity, are likely to derail the venture's success.

Chapter Conclusion

This chapter focused on decisions Crassus made after escaping Rome. Crassus independently raised a 2,500-man army and personally backed the undertaking, but he was accused of plundering a Spanish coastal town. After disagreeing with a more senior Metellus Pius in Africa, Crassus was determined to maintain control of his resources, and he did so by traveling with his troops directly to Sulla. Crassus played a crucial role for Sulla in the battle for Rome, but Plutarch disparaged him for the supposed plunder of an Italian town. Two modern lessons in entrepreneurial thinking are formulated in this chapter from Crassus' actions in Spain and in Africa:

Lesson 1: Envisage Your Future

Lesson 2: Control Your Future

The young Crassus showed three key attributes of entrepreneurial thinking in his decisions that support this chapter's lessons:

1. **Vision**

    In Spain, Crassus was prepared with a vision for the short term (revenge), and possibly for the long term (replenishment of family wealth and glory as a path to power), when he began to ally himself with Sulla.

2. **Flexibility**

    Crassus showed the flexibility to adjust his vision's details in Africa and sail to Sulla after falling out with Metellus.

3. **Tenacity**

    Crassus maintained sufficient control over his resources to help ensure successful implementation of his vision.

In this chapter, we saw Plutarch accuse Crassus of ignoring the wellbeing of the local population (the Malacans) to meet his goal to align with Sulla and of accumulating booty at his troops' expense (in Tuder). If only one of these two incidents is true, we have our first unseemly reflection of the robber barons in the actions of a young Crassus with power in his hands—self-interest trumps all.

The end justifying the means approach Crassus demonstrated fits in any robber baron's defense of his questionable activities, perhaps most clearly seen during Cornelius Vanderbilt's consolidation of railroad lines beginning in the 1860s. In the winter of 1867, during a bitter dispute with another railroad line, Vanderbilt stopped all connections with his competitor, effectively blockading Manhattan, and he "cut New York (State) off from the country" (Stiles 2010, 434).[14] As a result, Vanderbilt was later accused of dismissing others' welfare with the following statement, "What do I care about the law? Ain't I got the power?" T. J. Stiles, Vanderbilt's biographer, discovered that Vanderbilt never uttered these words attributed to him. However, Stiles discovered that, during a New York State Legislative hearing on the "blockade" matter, Vanderbilt said, "The law, as I view it, goes too slow for me when I have the remedy in my own hands . . ." (Stiles 2010, 434).[15] Vanderbilt's attitude toward achieving his goal, much like that of

Crassus, eclipsed concerns for collateral damage to others, even disinterested parties in the underlying dispute.

Figure 1.9. Reports of a Vanderbilt dismissing the public's welfare reached new heights in 1882, as caricatured by Fredrick Opper. In this cartoon, an overweight and self-satisfied William Vanderbilt, the Commodore's oldest son and principal heir, reclines in his office chair stating, "the public be damned" (a remark he made to a reporter). Chained to Vanderbilt's chair are two cowering dogs representing the US Congress and the New York State Legislature. An American eagle is also trampled under Vanderbilt's foot.

61

Chapter 2. Victory and Opportunity

Sulla's Policies

Sulla's defeat of his enemies in Rome ended the civil war, but he was brutal to his defeated adversaries. According to Plutarch, Sulla had a cowering Senate name him dictator, an office of the Republic that had not seen an occupant in more than 120 years, thus setting a precedent that Julius Caesar later followed. Plutarch in his biography of Sulla describes the horrible fury of his vengeance (Plutarch, *Sulla* 31):

> *Sulla now began to make blood flow, and he filled the city with deaths without number or limit; many persons were murdered on grounds of private enmity, who had never had anything to do with Sulla, but he consented to their death to please his adherents. At last, a young man, Caius Metellus, had the boldness to ask Sulla in the Senate-house, when there would be an end to these miseries and how far he would proceed before they could hope to see them stop. "We are not deprecating," he said, "your vengeance against those whom you have*

The public communication of those enemies to be "punished" by Sulla was known as *the list of the proscribed*. To be *proscribed* meant that you were publicly declared an enemy of the state and subject to immediate execution. The State then confiscated the victim's assets and put them up for sale at a public auction. Anyone who tried to protect the proscribed, father, mother, wife, daughter, or son was put to death. The bounty for killing a proscribed person was two talents of gold (a bounty of almost $4 million today), paid to whoever did the killing.

But death alone did not end the punishment for those Sulla proscribed. Plutarch also tells us that Sulla prohibited the sons *and* grandsons of the proscribed from political office and confiscated their inheritances (Plutarch, *Sulla* 31). Sulla's proscriptions were carried out not just in the city of Rome, but also across all Italy, possibly affecting nine thousand people (Everitt 2003, 41).[1]

A much more modern and enlightened approach to dealing with the defeated in a civil war is found in Abraham Lincoln's approach to the Confederacy in the days immediately preceding Robert E. Lee's surrender in the American Civil War. Lincoln advised one of his generals (Godfrey Weitzel) to "let 'em up easy" (Perret 2004, 403; Sandburg 1939, 227)[2] and even visited wounded Confederate soldiers (Perret 2004, 404).[3]

Lincoln did not live to carry out his intended policy. Sulla had no such intention to let his enemies "up easy" and instead carried out revenge diametrically opposed to the strategy Lincoln favored. Then, Lincoln had the benefit of 1,900 years of hindsight, for he read Plutarch's *Lives* in 1860, which described Sulla's actions after his victory in his civil war (Tarbell 2012, 71).[4]

Crassus and the Sullan Policy of Proscription

With the victory of Sulla's forces and the resultant proscriptions, we come to the next major milestone for Crassus that affected both the course of his life (his wealth and power) and his legacy (his reputation for avarice). But before we begin our study of this period of Crassus' career, let's look more closely at his family life before the start of the civil war to better understand his desire for vengeance and possibly gain insight into what drove Crassus' actions in the period immediately after the end of the Sullan civil war.

Plutarch is quick to tell his readers that Crassus was raised in a "small" house (Plutarch, *Crassus* 1), and he continued to live there with his mother, father (who had once been consul of Rome besides serving as a provincial governor), and two married brothers until the bloodshed of the civil war intervened. Plutarch even reports they all ate at the same table. He likely wanted to emphasize the yawning chasm between the great wealth Crassus accumulated and his modest beginnings, but in the process, he reveals that Crassus had a close relationship with his immediate family.

Before the civil war began, an older brother of Crassus died, and Crassus married his brother's widow (Tertulla). This might have been done to avoid the necessity of returning her dowry, but Crassus, unlike many of his senatorial peers, stayed married to his wife for the rest of his life, and with Tertulla, raised two sons (Publius and Marcus).

After the outbreak of the civil war, Cinna and his loyalists were responsible for the death of Crassus' surviving brother and for his father's suicide. Making matters worse, Crassus' father's head was hung in Rome's city center. Those responsible for the death of his father and brother could not go unpunished, and Crassus had no pity for his defeated enemies. Thus, Crassus had no qualms about Sulla's policy of proscription—his complete support of the program is not open to debate.

Plutarch Comments on Crassus' Behavior

Plutarch (*Crassus* 6) tells us that during the period of proscriptions, a hard-hearted Crassus "got a bad name, by buying at low prices large properties" of the proscribed at public auctions. This comment by Plutarch is critical to both the historic depiction of Crassus as rapacious and insightful into his approach to business— Crassus had the steely determination to exploit the opportunity Sulla's (and his own) vengeance offered.

All among Sulla's officer corps and circle of friends would have been encouraged to buy the victims' property. Often, those purchases were made at bargain basement prices because the properties were typically sold at auction, and if Sulla's favorites were bidding, others bowed out for fear they, too, might find their names added to the proscription lists.

The Additional Benefits of Proscriptions for Sulla

The Roman nobility long considered *booty*, or spoils of war, a legitimate means to gain wealth, and Sulla rationalized that his enemies, even though they were Roman citizens, were traitors to the state; therefore, their assets qualified as booties. Thus, Sulla could, as any victorious Roman general did, reward his loyalists with a share of the booties, allowing them to recoup or grow family fortunes, and even more important, tie them all the more closely to him and his regime.

That Plutarch called out Crassus for buying multiple properties perhaps shows less his desire for revenge (as the proscribed, in most instances, were already dead) than an insight into his entrepreneurial thinking. Crassus likely wanted to enhance his family's "modest" wealth and resolved that the best opportunity to do so was through acquiring his executed enemies' large estates, just as Sulla would have wanted.

Other Sullan loyalists had the same opportunity but failed to emulate the scope of Crassus' actions, perhaps to avoid the odor of such purchases, a risk Crassus was willing to accept. Remember, the properties were sold at auction—public auctions—so there was no hiding purchases from the deceased's families, your peers, or the public.

Crassus' Commitment to Large Property Purchases

Crassus was decisive (although with a decisiveness initially fed by vengeance) about the size of his investment in a real estate market when others might have wavered because of the potential risks:

1. Risk that a purchase at some future date might be overturned in Rome's law courts or the possibility of retribution from the proscribed's family or friends when Sulla departed the scene.

2. Risk that the perception of the purchase or purchases was tainted and would negatively impact the buyer's reputation (as did happen to Crassus' reputation *and* also his long-term legacy).

Crassus' decision to invest in many large properties, despite all the associated risks, when others passed on the opportunity, establishes our third lesson to extract from Crassus' actions.

Lesson 3. Carefully Assess Risk/Reward Tradeoffs

Crassus accepted the risks associated with becoming a large buyer of the proscribed's property, and his reputation definitely suffered for that decision. Crassus must have decided that the short-term benefits, such as revenge and maintaining Sulla's support by publicly showing commitment to the hated program of proscriptions, and the longer-term potential for significant profit "outweighed" the risks (figure 2.1).

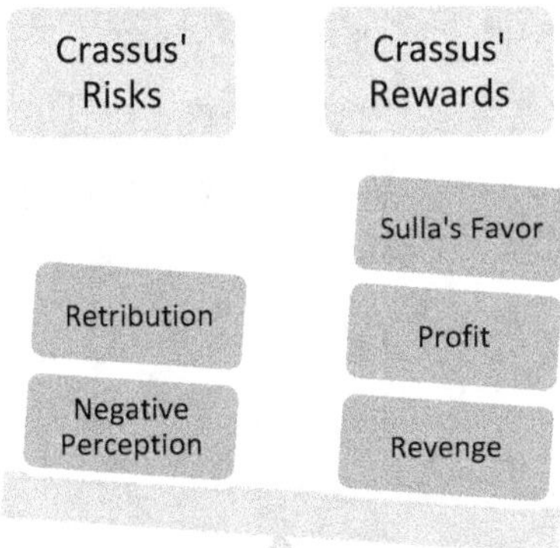

Figure 2.1. When buying the proscribed's property, there were both risks and rewards for Crassus to consider.

The Ethics of Crassus' Purchases

Crassus was apparently unbothered by the risks associated with his purchases of property of the proscribed. Was Crassus immoral in his decision? Sulla controlled the reins of government and the lives of the men he defeated as well as their property (which he deemed war booties). Despite the distastefulness of Crassus' actions to our modern senses, Roman law sanctioned them.

Another "Modern" Example from the American Civil War

After Lincoln's assassination, harsh treatment of the defeated can be found after the North's victory in the American Civil War. At the end of the war, so-called *carpetbaggers* (figure 2.2) traveled from the North to the South and bought many great plantations at distressed prices from their destitute owners. They then hired the recently freed slaves to work the newly acquired plantations. Some carpetbaggers were even elected to Congress in their new home states, and the term is still in use (both Bobby Kennedy and Hillary Clinton were called carpetbaggers for moving to New York state and running for the US Senate). History repeating does not excuse immoral behavior, but it reminds us that businesspersons and the companies they run are only required to play by the rules the state enforces.

Figure 2.2. An 1872 cartoon of a carpetbagger (suitcases at the time were made of carpet). Caricatured is Carl Schurz, who at the time was a US senator from Missouri.

The actions of Crassus, in purchasing forfeited properties, and the carpetbaggers who came after the American Civil War, are not an argument for following instructions to do what you find unethical, even if legal. Instead, they are an important reminder to avoid (despite the difficulty in doing so) those actions, even under social pressure, that could cause your straying from your moral compass.

In Crassus' case, we must admit that he seems morally unbothered by his chosen path. He more likely believed his vendetta was honorable and even required because of the violence done to his family and the state, for the usual Roman punishment for murder was death to the perpetrator, although aristocrats in many such instances could choose exile.

So, should we condemn Crassus for doing what he and all other Sullan loyalists were allowed, expected, and perhaps even required to do? Ancient Rome was a different time and a different place, operating under different standards from the modern world, and if Crassus' side had lost, he would have faced consequences identical to those inflicted on Sulla's enemies. Sulla's proscriptions were not criminal, but Sulla's adversaries were made criminals under Roman law, and so their punishment by Sulla, as protector of the state, though harsh, was legal and would be replicated with equal enthusiasm by future Roman generations.

Entrepreneurs and Risk

Having discussed Crassus' ethical standards (or lack of), let's now look at his willingness to accept risk. Crassus ignored the public's perception of his actions and accepted the risks associated with his aggressive acquisition of property from Sulla's long list of the proscribed. Is Crassus' apparent comfort with significant risk typical of most modern entrepreneurs (who are not typically dealing in bloodstained properties)? The opinion of most interested observers today would be yes, that entrepreneurs comprise a unique club of risktakers. However, that opinion, at least in one study, is more myth than reality, and entrepreneurs are typically as uncomfortable with significant risk as most upper-level managers in the private sector.

Research in a 1998 study presented at the Babson College Entrepreneurship Research Conference by John W. Mullins, University of Denver, and David Forlani, University of Colorado at Denver, revealed that successful entrepreneurs showed themselves as risk-averse as typical business managers. The researchers compared the responses of thirty-nine entrepreneurs (running fast-growing public companies with revenues of $9 million to $1.2 billion) with twenty-five upper-level managers attending a Midwestern university's executive education program. The respondents were asked to evaluate four theoretical business ventures, each with varying risk and rewards. The differences in the respondents' risk perception were not statistically significant, and they are shown in table 2.1 (where 7 is the maximum perceived risk).

Table 2.1. Managers' Risk-Aversion Compared with Entrepreneurs' Risk-Aversion (Copyright 1998 Babson College).

Venture	Managers' Perceived Risk	Entrepreneurs' Perceived Risk
A	5.12	5.95
B	4.39	4.65
C	3.55	3.43
D	2.04	1.89

It should be noted that discomfort with risk in no way means that once the scale tilts in favor of rewards over risks, an entrepreneur will not commit wholeheartedly, just as Crassus proceeded to aggressively acquire the property of the proscribed despite the inherent risks (although those unique risks were a direct result of Sulla's programmatic destruction of his and Crassus' enemies).

Criticism of Crassus Compared with Sulla

Plutarch indicates that Crassus was much more compelled by his lust for the proscribed's property than in his pursuit of vengeance, and as a result, comes in for much harsher criticism than Sulla, his superior, does. Crassus is reviled for intending to make money at his dead enemies' expense, whereas Sulla stayed focused on just extracting his bloody revenge—apparently a much more tolerable vice than greed. Plutarch also reports that long after Sulla died, Cicero even used the public posting of Sulla's proscription lists in a joke about Sulla's son. For when Sulla's grown son "got into debt and squandered most of his substance, (and) advertised his household stuff for sale" (Plutarch, *Cicero* 27), Cicero quipped that he much preferred the son's posting to that of the father.

The Value of Crassus' Purchases

Perhaps we should take a moment to understand the potential scale of some real estate transactions arising from Sulla's proscriptions. A number of villas were sold in the Roman Republic's heated real estate market during the last century before the birth of Christ, and ancient authors felt compelled to document the prices of a few palatial homes of Rome's senators.

Documented home sale prices ranged from 3,500,000 to more than 14,000,000 sesterces, where a sesterce can be thought of as roughly equivalent to $4 today (using today's value of gold as our conversion standard). Therefore, the values of the palatial villas of Republican Rome would be estimated at $14 million–$56 million each! Because of the number of senators proscribed, we can assume that some homes of great size, with exquisite locations and of significant value, were included in the auctions and, therefore, purchased by Crassus.

The Price of Crassus' Purchases

The sale price of homes sold at auction is much more difficult to assess. We know from one of Cicero's court cases in 80 BC that an estate of thirteen farms fifty miles north of Rome in Umbria, many of which bordered the Tiber River (benefiting transport), was worth a cumulative 6,000,000 sesterces, or about $24 million today. The total estate was sold at auction for just 2,000 sesterces, or about $8,000 today (Cicero, *Pro Roscius Amerinus;* Ward 1977, 66).[5] The buyer was a powerful henchman of Sulla, a freedman (ex-slave) named Lucius Cornelius Chrysogonus.

Whether the price Chrysogonus paid was the trend or an aberration, we do not know, but we can assume that when Sulla's most powerful supporters sought prime properties, the opportunity for competitive bidding was limited. Whether Crassus fell into this select category is unknown because that data is unavailable to us.

Because proscriptions had the dual purpose of exacting revenge *and* replenishing the treasury, not all great pieces of property could have been sold at fire-sale prices.

Two Examples of Grand Roman Villas

We do not have images of the properties Crassus purchased, but to illustrate, two examples of palatial Roman villas are provided in figures 2.3 and 2.4. The first, shown in figure 2.3, is The Getty Villa in Malibu, CA whose physical design was drawn from the Villa of the Papyri, a villa in the town of Herculaneum, which, along with Pompeii, was destroyed by Mt. Vesuvius' eruption in AD 79.

Figure 2.3. The Getty Villa's design gives a sense of what a palatial "rural" villa Crassus purchased might have resembled (Copyright © Rolf_52/shutterstock.com).

The ancient villa's front extended for more than 2,500 feet and overlooked what is now the Bay of Naples.

The second, shown in figure 2.4 (one of many reconstructions), is from a mid-nineteenth century drawing of a Tuscan villa owned by the Roman Senator Pliny the Younger (c. AD 61–AD 112/3), based on Pliny's detailed description of it (Pliny, Letters 6).

Figure 2.4. An 1842 reconstruction by Karl Friedrich of the Tuscan villa owned by Pliny the Younger, a Roman senator and consul in AD 100. Crassus' wealth is estimated at ten times that of Pliny.

Additional Potential Purchases of Crassus

Plutarch provides little additional detail of Crassus' purchases during the proscriptions, but tells us that Crassus ultimately owned, besides villas:

1.   Silver and tin mines (some of which Crassus' father might have originally owned)
2.   Great tracts of farmland in the countryside
3.   Palatial homes in the city of Rome

All these physical assets required a substantial slave population to support their upkeep and operation to ensure their income production was maintained or grown. It seems unlikely that the remote properties would have been sold separately from their supporting slave populations. (We see in later chapters that Crassus was also a large buyer of slaves.) Although it is feasible that auctioned property in Rome was sold as a lot distinct from the slaves, increasing income for the state, even when the houses were sold inexpensively.

The purchase and maintenance of the great homes in the city of Rome, unlike income-producing properties such as mines and farms, would have drained Crassus' funds, or that of any other buyers, as they were net consumers of cash. Therefore, Crassus possibly bought so many city properties he became strapped for money and perhaps even had to borrow to fund his acquisitiveness (Adcock 1966. 16).[6] Crassus' steadfast commitment to his real estate investment strategy forms the basis of our fourth lesson from the entrepreneurial thinking of Crassus.

Lesson 4. Have the Courage of Your Convictions

Crassus, once having decided his acquisitive course, proceeded aggressively to buy property. These acquisitions occurred although Crassus' inherited wealth was modest compared with other noble families and that Cinna and his allies confiscations might also have diminished Crassus' family wealth (Ward 1977, 48, n. 11).[7]

Crassus, perhaps more than any other supporter of Sulla, likely went short on cash and long on property. Crassus' decision was ethically questionable. However, that decision was unmistakably financially and politically rewarding, for Crassus' determination to buy properties rapidly produced great wealth and launched Crassus on his power path. Thus, we can state with little controversy that Crassus is probably one of history's poster boys for the Machiavellian maxim that the end justifies the means.

Crassus' Gamble Pays Off Big

Shortly after his military victory, Sulla named 125 men, most likely chosen from his officer corps, to fill open seats in the 300-man

Roman Senate depleted by death, war, and his proscriptions (Keaveney 2005, 145).[8] This major wave of entrants probably included Crassus (Pompey the Great was still too young to qualify for the Senate, which required an age of at least 30). Sulla also resolved to increase the aggregate number of senators from 300 to 600 (Keaveney 2005, 145), which would dramatically affect Crassus' real estate holdings.[9] A critical element of senatorial status was owning a palatial home in Rome's city center, and Crassus now had more than he could use for himself.

Because Plutarch tells us elsewhere that when Crassus died, a significant part of his wealth was still contained in great estates outside the city proper, Crassus likely kept the income-producing rural estates and sold several of the city mansions he purchased in what was a "buyers' market" at a significant profit. This attention to the details of the real estate market in which Crassus competed forms the basis for this chapter's final lesson in entrepreneurial thinking:

Lesson 5. Know Your Brief

With new status-conscious senators competing with one another for the appropriately grandiose home, the high-end real estate market rapidly transformed into a "sellers' market," and no one was better positioned to prosper by the transformation than

Crassus was. An understanding of Rome's property market, close attention to the Senate's vacancy rate, and thinking through the implications of Sulla's decision to increase the Senate's size (which may have been shared with selected Sullan insiders) reduced the long-term financial risk of Crassus' large real estate investments. Crassus' apparent diligence also yielded significant returns much more quickly than other potential buyers might have assumed. Perhaps Crassus was not just the most aggressive and consistent buyer, but also the most sensitive to factors affecting the market in which he took part.

A Legacy Tarnished by a Contemporary

Crassus made enormous amounts of money on his real estate bets. However, one major risk accompanying the purchase of property from the proscribed was the potential impact on your reputation. Crassus came in for much criticism much later from Plutarch, but one of Crassus' most vocal and damaging critics was also one of his real estate clients.

For in 62 BC, Crassus, who was still selling prestigious homes nearly two decades after Sulla's proscriptions ended, sold Cicero "one of the grandest mansions in the city's grandest quarter, the Palatine Hill, overlooking the Forum" (Everitt 1999, 115).[10] Cicero, in one of his surviving letters to a friend, gleefully reported that

Crassus sold him the mansion at the bargain price of 3,500,000 sesterces, or about $14 million (Cicero, *Friends* 6.2). We saw this same Cicero enthusiastically linking the less attractive personality traits of Crassus and Sulla. We also find that Cicero was quick to condemn businessmen when he wrote that they should be "rejected as undesirable" (Cicero, *On Duties* I.150).

Cicero's hypocritical approach to Crassus—to privately avail himself of one of Crassus' stable of prestigious properties while publicly condemning him—did not stop with the above example. While Crassus was alive, Cicero directly promised him "exemplary devotion in every kind of service" (Cicero, *Friends* 25.4). But after Crassus was killed in battle, Cicero wrote of Crassus that if "one were to offer a Marcus Crassus the power, that by the mere snapping of his fingers, to get himself named as an heir (to a large inheritance), when he was not really an heir, he would, I warrant you, dance in the forum" (Cicero, *On Duties* III.75).

Cicero's belated criticism of Crassus still yielded a very effective threefold putdown of the dead Crassus:

1.   Cicero implied that Crassus was so greedy that he would stoop to immoral behavior and intentionally misappropriate an inheritance.

2.   Cicero implied that ill-gotten money would bring such joy to Crassus that he would not be embarrassed to gleefully dance in the forum.

3.   Cicero implied that for money, Crassus would demonstrate a businessman's lack of stature because respectable aristocrats viewed dancing as the preserve of the lower classes, women, and the sufficiently inebriated (figure 2.5).

Figure 2.5. An ancient Roman copy of a Greek relief of maenads, intoxicated women who were devotees of the god of wine, Dionysus, publicly dancing. (Copyright Timur Kulgarin/Shutterstock.com).

Cicero's criticisms of Crassus were a rich source for Plutarch, and for the last twenty centuries both men have done much to contribute to the lasting characterization of Crassus as innately avaricious and unscrupulous.

A Legacy Further Tarnished

Plutarch further condemns Crassus by citing an egregious instance of Crassus' supposed unethical behavior during the proscriptions. This example appears in Plutarch's biography of Crassus with no other known ancient source available for its corroboration (Ward 1977, 66).[11]

Plutarch reports that Crassus, without Sulla's authority, proscribed a man from Bruttium (modern Calabria, figure 2.6) more than 300 miles south of Rome near the toe of Italy.

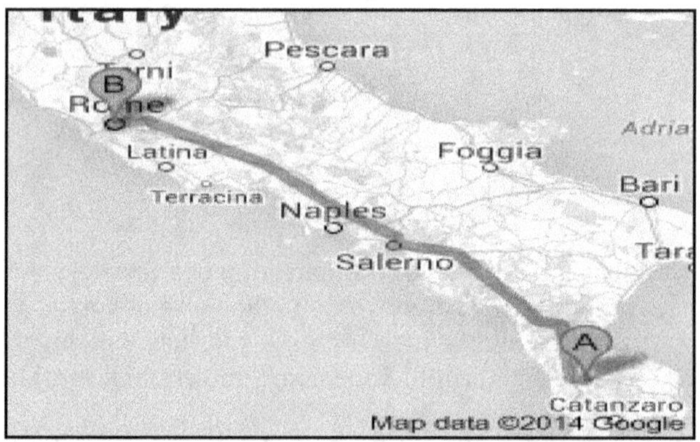

Figure 2.6. Shows the more than 300-mile distance between Rome (B) and Bruttium, now modern Calabria (A), where, according to Plutarch, Crassus had a man proscribed without Sulla's approval.

According to Plutarch, Crassus proscribed the man "not pursuant to Sulla's orders, but merely to enrich himself thereby, and that, on this account, Sulla, who disapproved of his conduct, never employed him again in any public business" (Plutarch, *Crassus* 6).

This example is so odious that we cannot help wonder why Cicero (despite his protestations to the contrary), Pompey, or any other of Crassus' political adversaries, would not have used the event Plutarch described to smear Crassus while he was alive. (This would have possibly provided Plutarch and us an opportunity to see how Crassus defended himself from this accusation as he did with the claim that he plundered the Malacans.) Unfortunately, despite the absence of any corroboration, this account of Crassus' illicit behavior is crucial to the historic depiction of Crassus. If accurate, he was greedy *and* venal; if untrue, his reputation was unfairly tarnished, and perhaps he should have "just" been labeled an excessively avaricious man.

Was Crassus Capable?

Although Cicero is silent on this incident involving Crassus, we know that in 80 BC, a then 26-year-old Cicero, in his first public criminal trial, won great fame defending a wrongfully proscribed man's son. An Umbrian man was killed for his wealth by cousins, who then had the dead man proscribed. When the act was discovered, the perpetrators attempted to frame the man's son for his father's murder (Cicero, Defense Speeches, *Pro Roscius Amerinus*). This all took place to steal an estate worth 6,000,000 sesterces. (This is the same Umbrian estate auctioned for 2,000 sesterces and discussed earlier in this chapter.)

According to Cicero, Chrysogonus accomplished the post-murder proscription without Sulla's knowledge in return for a lion's share of the properties (Cicero, *Pro Roscius Amerinus* 20–22). If Chrysogonus could administratively make an illegal proscription without Sulla's consent, Crassus theoretically could have done just what Plutarch accused him of doing.

In this same trial, Cicero, after verbally eviscerating Sulla's powerful ex-slave, said, "For everyone is well aware that many people have committed many crimes, which Lucius Sulla, being preoccupied with his important public duties, either disapproved of or knew nothing about" (Cicero, *Pro Roscius Amerinus* 130). With this statement, Cicero hoped to protect himself from Sulla's wrath, but by exonerating Sulla of any foreknowledge of the crimes, Cicero sets forth the possibility, for us, that Plutarch's charge against Crassus is certainly credible.

To further re-enforce Plutarch's claim, we should note, "that Sulla had placed Crassus in charge of carrying out part of the proscriptions instituted at the beginning of his rule" (Ward 1977,

66).[12] Thus, we see that not only could illegitimate proscriptions be made, but also that Crassus was well positioned to do so.

Was Crassus Culpable?

Given his involvement in Roscius' trial, it is difficult to believe Cicero would have remained silent if there were any sign of Crassus having involved himself in such a fraudulent scheme as Plutarch described. At least according to some scholars, Cicero referenced an occasion where Crassus used a pseudonym (Calvus) to purchase a proscribed man's property (Cicero, *Atticus* I.16.5; Marshall 1976, 183).[13] So, Cicero's silence offers weight on the side of Crassus' innocence. But silence, especially when so many ancient voices have been lost because of time, does not provide a strong defense; so, let's examine motives why Crassus would undertake such a despicable action.

Plutarch's position is clear—Crassus was greedy—case closed; but if we are to search more deeply, we must explore three potential motives: revenge, a favor, and greed. Was revenge for his father's death a driver here? Not likely, because Bruttium was so far from Rome, and Cinna and his cohorts were from Rome's nobility, not of remote Italian stock. If the motive were vengeance, why didn't Crassus go to Sulla, who seemed to have no qualms about executing his enemies and those of his loyalists? Therefore, vengeance seems not to be the motive here.

Could Crassus have committed the act as a favor for another? Perhaps, but if so, it mitigates nothing, for committing an illegal act for another was no better than Crassus doing it for himself. The favor would need to be repaid at some point, and thus, Crassus would still benefit from an act of premeditated murder.

We next come to Plutarch's motive of simple greed. Today, modern Calabria is still known for its lush, beautiful *and ancient* olive orchards, so perhaps in antiquity, Crassus wanted to have a grand olive-growing estate. Of course, it was hundreds of miles from Rome, and he had been busy fighting a bloody war, overseeing proscriptions for Sulla, buying and operating multiple urban and rural properties, managing his mining interests with their extensive slave populations, and reuniting with his family after his long absence. Given what Crassus already had on his plate, it is difficult, at first glance, to imagine his developing such an intense acquisitiveness for so remote a location that he would risk incurring Sulla's wrath. However, Professor Arthur Keaveney, in his definitive biography of Sulla, writes that Sulla, as part of the proscription process, appointed Crassus as head of a commission that "went on circuit to make a scrutiny of men's loyalties." (Keaveney 2005, 126).[14] Such a position could have brought

Crassus to Bruttium and might explain how he came to covet an estate so distant from Rome.

So, if all that then stood between Crassus and the property's ownership was, as Cicero claimed in the court case involving Chrysogonus, keeping the deed from the busy dictator, Bruttium's remoteness made the probability of Crassus' discovery by Sulla far from certain, and it makes the potential for Crassus' culpability, as recorded by Plutarch, the more likely.

Why Run the Risk?

Plutarch in his biography of Sulla describes the dictator as violent, vain, and inhuman—a tyrant and a butcher. Plutarch also writes, "The sales of confiscated property were conducted by him (Sulla) from his tribunal" (Plutarch, *Sulla* 32). Therefore, even if Crassus' fraudulent proscription could be done secretly, the illegitimately auctioned property might still come to Sulla's attention. Why would Crassus dare risk crossing such a man as Sulla?

Earlier in the text, we saw Sulla order Crassus to raise troops in enemy territory without the protection of any guards, and Crassus did as Sulla ordered him, even though it placed his life in danger. No matter how special a property the remote Bruttium estate could have been, would its possession, given all Crassus had achieved and acquired under Sulla, be worth the risk of a relationship breach or worse?

Although precise timelines are difficult to establish, early in the proscription process, Sulla likely anointed Pompey as Magnus (the Great) and engaged his stepdaughter to him. This elevation of Pompey might have spurred Crassus to risk his alliance with Sulla, because he thought he was left in the cold of Pompey's elongating shadow.

Perhaps jealousy of Pompey's relationship with Sulla and even anger at Sulla himself induced Crassus to do as Chrysogonus did and as Plutarch accuses. Possibly the risk of a breach with Sulla would merely damage an already-eroding relationship, and it was not so risky as to be fatal. After all, Chrysogonus went unpunished (beyond public humiliation) for his role in the illicit proscription. One last point against Crassus' innocence—because Sulla appointed Crassus to oversee the proscriptions *only in the early stages,* we have support for Plutarch's claim that Sulla punished Crassus by not employing him in any public business again (Plutarch, *Crassus* 6). Despite all the discussion here, we cannot know with any certainty whether the events occurred as Plutarch reported, but Plutarch's position on the matter is at least as strong, if not stronger, as the silence of Crassus' contemporaries on his supposed crime of falsely proscribing a man to obtain a much-desired, olive-growing property.

Chapter Conclusion

As seen in this chapter, Crassus' behavior was unsavory, even by ancient standards, both during the period that immediately followed Sulla's victory in the civil war and during his dictatorship that followed. However, from Crassus' brutal form of entrepreneurialism demonstrated during the period of the proscriptions, we constructed three useful (and much more benign) lessons for the modern workplace:

Lesson 3: Carefully Assess Risk/Reward Tradeoffs

Lesson 4: Have the Courage of Your Convictions

Lesson 5: Know Your Brief

Two attributes of entrepreneurial thinking are apparent in Crassus' aggressive and morally repulsive response to the property sales the Sullan confiscations made available:

1. **Confidence**

   Crassus demonstrated the confidence to make critical decisions, despite the risks to his reputation.

2. **Passion**

   Although initially fed by vengeance, and then profit, Crassus showed a bloody passion that ensured he did

not waver from his chosen course of using the assets
of the legally (and perhaps illegally) proscribed to fuel
his campaign for money, property, and power.

The Robber Baron Attitude

For two millennia, Crassus has been criticized for his actions
during Sulla's bloody period of proscriptions, which included
capitalizing on the dead's assets. Those actions were not unique to
Crassus or ancient Rome, as we saw in discussing the carpetbaggers
exploiting the misery after the American Civil War.

Modern robber barons, who reached the apogee of their power
during the decades following the American Civil War, would likely
have applauded Crassus' actions. Although we do not know with
any certainty, we can infer their approval by a quote representative
of the robber barons' actions that is attributed to John D.
Rockefeller, the richest of them all and one of the richest men in
history. Rockefeller coldly advised, "The way to make money is to
buy when blood is on the streets." Crassus certainly made money
when blood literally was on the streets.

Figure 2.7. A 1901 Puck cartoon portraying Rockefeller as a steely-eyed emperor standing on a pedestal labeled Standard Oil and wearing a golden crown of all the industries that comprised his dominions.

Crassus was much maligned for the palatial houses he acquired, but in his case, the grand properties were a means to an end—increasing his wealth. The robber barons constructed great estates because they wanted to live in a fashion commensurate with their wealth.

Perhaps the best example of the extravagance that epitomizes the robber baron passion for palatial properties can be found in the "home" Cornelius Vanderbilt's grandson constructed between 1889 and 1895. Known as *the Biltmore Estate*, the mansion has 250 rooms, and it was constructed on 125,000 acres in North Carolina. The home is America's largest at more than 175,000 square feet, and it remains in the Vanderbilt family today.

Figure 2.8. The 250-room Biltmore Estate Cornelius Vanderbilt's grandson, George, constructed in the 1880s. (Copyright Fotoluminate LLC/Shutterstock.com.)

Chapter 3. Fire and Opportunity

Rome and Conflagrations

Plutarch, in his steady drumbeat of Crassus' unnatural love for money, emphasizes that most of Crassus' wealth came from exploiting the victims of "fire and the war" (Plutarch, *Crassus* 2). We discussed the victims of war (the proscribed) in the previous chapter, so now, we must examine how Crassus came to prey on the victims of fire.

Rome in the last century BC was one of the most densely populated and congested cities of antiquity, with an estimated population of at least one million people (Stambaugh 1988, 89).[1] By comparison, New York City did not reach a population of one million until the 1870s, with Manhattan's land area alone exceeding twenty-two square miles. Rome's population was packed into less than three square miles, a geographic area protected and bounded by the Servian Walls, which were constructed in the early fourth century BC (figure 3.1). By AD 275, the Aurelian Walls, which encompassed a bit more than five square miles (figures 3.1 and 3.2), protected the city's residents.

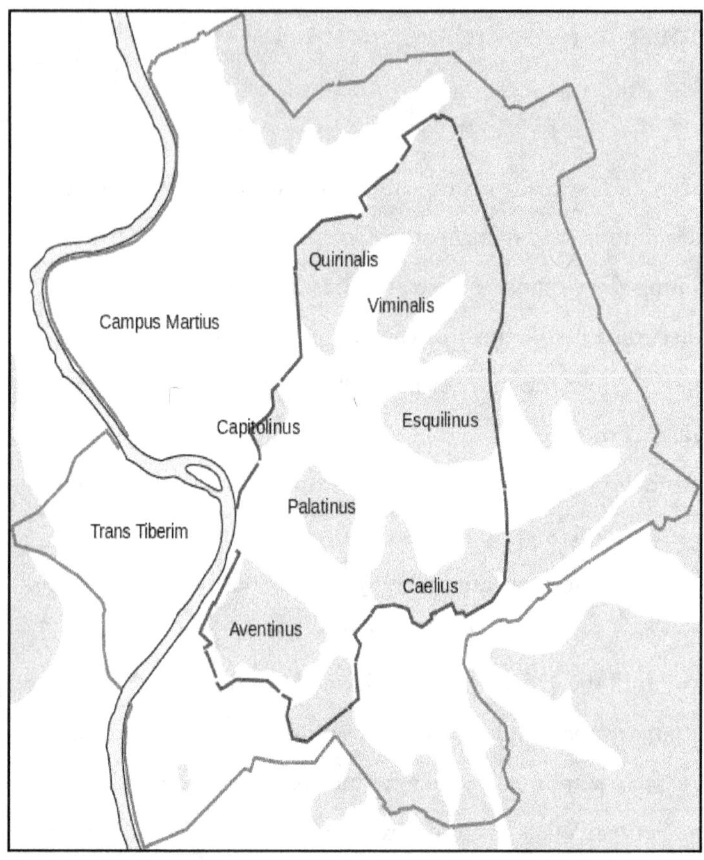

Figure 3.1. Map of the ancient city of Rome and its Seven Hills protected by the Servian Walls (inner lines), which had a perimeter of seven miles and were built during the fourth century BC. This figure also shows the enlarged Aurelian Walls (outer lines) built in AD 275, which had a twelve-mile perimeter.

Figure 3.2. Segment of the monolithic Aurelian Walls in Rome today. Notice how the wall dwarfs a parked car.

Housing Structures

Housing structures during the Republican period were jammed with shops on the narrow streets and often rose to six or seven stories. The buildings were constructed cheaply, primarily built of wood and mud bricks. Later, during the Empire, the dwellings were more frequently built of fired bricks (figure 3.3) and were structurally sounder, as the Emperor Augustus instituted height restrictions on new buildings. As a testimony to his improving the Empire's architectural standards, the Emperor Augustus boasted, "I found Rome of clay; I leave it to you of marble" (Dio, *Roman History* 56.30).

Figure 3.3. The remains of a brick apartment building of the Imperial period that still stands in Rome today.

The wooden buildings of Crassus' time were subject to collapse, and if the structures avoided that calamity, they often caught fire because candles and oil-burning lamps (figure 3.4) provided light, and the same open brazier used for cooking provided heat in cold weather. Adjacent shops storing flammable material, such as olive oil and grain, only exacerbated the fire risk.

Figure 3.4. The open flame of an ancient oil lamp.
(Copyright Yingko/Shutterstock.com.)

A further significant contributing factor to the risk of fire was that there were only limited and inconsistently enforced building codes (building spacing, wall thickness, building height) to control landlords and to protect tenants (Canter 1931, 286).[2] There were also no insurance companies to offer their unique form of protection to the owners or to the tenants. An AD fourth-century census showed there were about 47,000 tenements in Rome and 1,800 standalone mansions owned by the wealthy (Stambaugh 1988, 90; 338, n. 6).[3] Granted, this census was conducted more than 400 years after Crassus' death, but it is not unreasonable to expect the building counts and the ratio of the dwellings of the poor to those of the wealthy to stay constant, because the city's overall size did not change significantly (although by AD 400, the city was far along on its well-documented decline). These statistics are not intended to furnish an exact building count, rather to give a sense of the great number of tenements subject to the risk of fire and collapse in the Late Republic and to provide a sizing of the real estate "market" (both low-end and high) in which Crassus played such a significant role.

Crassus and Conflagrations

Crassus looked at Rome's vulnerability to conflagrations and saw a business opportunity others apparently hadn't noticed. Plutarch describes his nefarious moneymaking scheme:

> *Observing the accidents that were indigenous and familiar at Rome, conflagrations, and tumbling down of houses owing to their weight and crowded state, he (Crassus) bought slaves, who were architects and builders. Having got these slaves to the number of more than five hundred, it was his practice to buy up houses on fire, and the houses which were adjoining to those on fire for the owners, owing to fear and uncertainty, would sell them at a low price; and thus the greatest part of Rome fell into the hands of Crassus."* (Plutarch, *Crassus* 2)

We need to spend time analyzing this brief paragraph. Plutarch provides the underlying causes of building destruction—collapses because of (1) structure weight and their crowded state and (2) conflagrations.

Plutarch did not blame Crassus for either grievous calamity, but some modern "sources" have speculated that Crassus instructed his agents to start fires among the vulnerable wooden structures he wanted to acquire. For example, in discussing Crassus at the *Illustrated History of the Roman Empire* (*RomanEmpire.net* n.d.), we find the following statement: "There was no doubt some who wondered, if some of the fires started in Rome might not actually have been his doing."[4]

We know that our ancient source, Plutarch, did not wonder about Crassus' role in starting the fires, or he would have mentioned it along with all the other sins he recorded. However, the modern allegations do not stop there, for in the online pages of the *Ancient History™ Encyclopedia* (Mark 2009), we find an example of how low Crassus could supposedly go: "Crassus was the richest man in Rome and was corrupt to the point of forcing wealthy citizens to pay him 'safety' money. If the citizen paid, Crassus would not burn down that person's house but, if no money was forthcoming, the fire would be lighted and Crassus would then charge a fee to send men to put the fire out."[5]

Although we might detect very faint echoes of Plutarch's Crassus in modern depictions of Crassus' so-called *propensity* to start or threaten fires for personal gain, if we rely on Plutarch, we can assume Crassus was not running a "protection racket." He was also unlikely an entrepreneurial arsonist, especially given the Draconian penalties for intentionally starting a fire in Rome. In ancient Roman law (the Twelve Tables), the punishment for intentionally setting a fire was death by fire. This was the Emperor Nero's excuse in AD 64 for illuminating his gardens with burning Christians, whom he blamed for setting the Great Fire of Rome that destroyed much of the city. Crassus would have been under the threat of a painful death if he or his agents started fires on property he wished to acquire.

Crassus Capitalizes on the Outbreak of Fires

Given Plutarch's detailed statements about Crassus' fire-related activities, Crassus made it his practice to buy burning apartment houses and those in the surrounding area during the conflagrations. The negotiations would then have taken place while the dwelling owners were under maximum stress and looking to avoid financial ruin. From Crassus' opportunistic identification of both a business need (protecting a landlord's assets subject to loss from nearby building fires and/or salvaging remaining asset values if fire was consuming the landlord's structure) and an associated solution (purchasing assets at risk), we form our sixth lesson in entrepreneurial thinking:

Lesson 6. One Man's Problem Is Another's Business

Opportunity

Crassus saw the fires as a business opportunity; if he hadn't, the buildings most likely would have been destroyed and the owners' investment and tenants' homes turned to ash. If that were not the case, the dwelling owners would have had no rationale for selling to Crassus. Crassus, although opportunistic and exploitive of the seller's misfortune, likely offered a much better deal than watching your apartment house incinerate and then rebuilding from scratch.

The purchase of endangered buildings has helped blacken Crassus' legacy. However, Crassus' "construction brigade" has further increased the condemnation of Crassus for his willingness to take advantage of those suffering from a calamity rather than to assist when he had the means (the brigade) to help. Should Crassus have taken personal responsibility for putting out fires in the city? Crassus' fellow senators would have viewed such generosity as excessive, and even threatening, for such a magnanimous action would have been thought self-serving and a blatant attempt to buy public support.

In fact, around 26 BC, a Roman magistrate named Marcus Egnatius Rufus won significant public adulation for providing a private fire brigade's services, but he incurred Emperor Augustus' (figure 3.5) ire (Reynolds 1996, 21; 20–21, n. 2) for the move.[6]

Figure 3.5. The Emperor Augustus, Julius Caesar's grandnephew. He not only transformed Rome into a city of marble, but also created a fledgling fire brigade in 22 BC that was likely seen as a great improvement over hastily formed bucket brigades of family, friends, slaves, and neighbors.

Augustus must have recognized the benefit of forming a government-sponsored fire brigade, for four years later he formed a firefighting brigade with six hundred of his slaves (Dio, *Roman History* 53.24). Augustus was likely dissatisfied with his original fire brigades' performance, for in AD 6, he expanded the firefighting force to *seven thousand* freedmen and distributed *and* housed them around the city (Reynolds 1996 22–25).[7]

To pay for the cost of this public service, Augustus allocated a portion of a tax on the sale of slaves to fund his much-enlarged brigade. (See appendix B for a discussion of slave manumission and its associated tax). This brigade was called the *Vigiles Urbani*, which meant "watchmen of the city," and they functioned as both a police force and as firemen (Canter 1931, 287–288).[8] So, although a private fire brigade's deployment in Crassus' day might have been technically workable and popular, one senator could not have likely accomplished it, despite his wealth, without overcoming significant political challenges.

Firefighting Equipment

Plutarch went to Rome twice in his lifetime, and we might suspect he gained personal knowledge of the fire brigade equipment by being in the city. That equipment included hooks, ladders, axes, saws, ropes, and buckets (Canter 1931, 287).[9] The Vigiles were descriptively nicknamed "the little bucket fellows" (Reynolds 1996,14), and Crassus' construction brigade likely used equipment similar to that of the Vigiles.[10] However, in ancient Rome, more specialized firefighting equipment was also in use in varying periods, and two of these—centones and siphones—are discussed below. A third, the ballista, is discussed later in this chapter.

Centones were coarse blanket-like materials "made wet and spread over buildings to prevent these from taking fire" (Canter 1931, 288).[11] If Crassus intended to buy buildings threatened by fire, we might assume his construction brigade used centones, which could be easily transported to the fire.

Siphones, or "fire engines," were the most sophisticated and complex of ancient Rome's available firefighting technology. Horses would have pulled the fire engine to a reservoir of water. It seems logistically unlikely that such a device (figure 3.6) could have been rapidly moved great distances through Rome's congestion (day and night) to fight the fires as soon as they flared. More likely, the sipho (whose invention c. 250 BC is attributed to the Greek inventor Ctesibius) only found use under Augustus' reign when multiple fire engines could be pre-positioned in districts, with the men trained in their use and familiar with local water sources (Reynolds 1996, 94).[12]

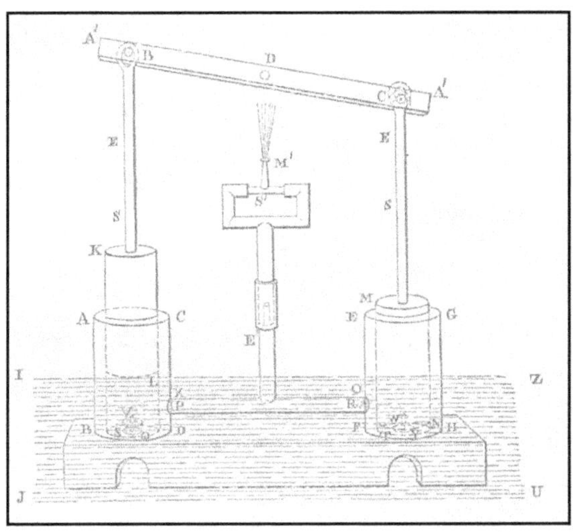

Figure 3.6. An illustration of an ancient Roman sipho submerged in water, based on ancient descriptions of the "fire engine." It's pump, thought to be double-action, forced the water out and toward the fire from the nozzle at position M'.

It is also not even clear whether siphones even existed for firefighting in Crassus' day. However, we know siphones were available for firefighting a century and a half later, in Rome, during Plutarch's lifetime (c. AD 100) because a Roman senator and Plutarch's contemporary, Pliny the Younger, lamented the absence of siphones in the provincial city of Nicomedia (in what is now Turkey). Writing in AD 110 to Emperor Trajan, Pliny complained, "There is not a single fire engine (sipho) anywhere in the town" (Pliny, *Letters* X.33.2).

107

Crassus' brigade size was limited (approximately five hundred compared with the seven thousand Augustus ultimately employed), and Plutarch does not mention Crassus' work crew being distributed around Rome (a practice Augustus found necessary for the force to be effective) or using specialized firefighting equipment. Given these facts and the political realities of the day, it is difficult to establish that Crassus' construction slaves made up a professional or dedicated firefighting force or that he failed to dispatch it in times of need.

No Competition for Crassus

Crassus' construction brigade, did however, bring him great wealth. As far as we know, no other aristocrat in Rome stepped forward with a construction brigade to compete with Crassus and capitalize on the business opportunity the highly flammable real estate market offered. Perhaps, other aristocrats desired not to sully their hands in this business or preferred to avoid competing with Crassus. The substantial start-up and operating costs involving the acquisition and ownership of hundreds of skilled slaves proved a significant barrier to entry, as even one slave in the Late Roman Republic could cost 500–8,000 sesterces or $2,000–$32,000 today (Horace, *Satire* II.7.43; *Epistle* II.2.5).

Another potential barrier to competition with Crassus was that acquiring, repairing, and flipping tenements in ancient Rome was not for the faint of heart, for flames take no notice of ownership, and all properties were vulnerable to fire, despite how exalted the owner's name (Ward 1977, 73).[13] Table 3.1 summarizes the potential barriers any competitor of Crassus might face.

Table 3.1. Barriers to Entry Competitors of Crassus Might Have Faced in Forming a Construction Brigade.

Barrier	Description
Start-up Costs	At a minimum of $2,000 a slave, the 500-plus slave brigade would have cost at least $1 million to form.
Operating Expenses	The entire slave brigade needed to be cared for (fed, clothed, housed) as long as the force existed.
Risk of Fire and Collapse	Once acquired, a tenement remained as vulnerable to fire and collapse as before it was purchased.
Peer Pressure	Every senator was sensitive to his dignity, and this form of wealth creation would not have been viewed as a positive.
Crassus' Wrath	Crassus continued to gain wealth and power, and he was not a man to be crossed lightly. A peer of Crassus described him as an ox that gored (Plutarch, *Crassus* 7).

We saw two modern examples of Crassus being charged with starting fires, but modern commentators also fixate on the image of Crassus himself with his firefighting brigade nearby, watching buildings burn if he was not paid to extinguish the fire. Here is one such example from *Wikipedia*'s History of Firefighting:[14]

> *One of his (Crassus') most lucrative schemes took advantage of the fact that Rome had no fire department. Crassus filled this void by creating his own brigade—500 men strong—which rushed to burning buildings at the first cry of alarm. Upon arriving at the scene, however, the firefighters did nothing while their employer bargained over the price of their services with the distressed property owner. If Crassus could not negotiate a satisfactory price, his men simply let the structure burn to the ground, after which he offered to purchase it for a fraction of its value.*

This example is another twist on Crassus and his construction brigade—Crassus offering firefighting *services for a fee*. Again, nothing of the sort is found in Plutarch, but given Crassus' penchant for exploiting the vulnerable, the creative Crassus was possibly the first to invent what is today called the "pay-or-pray" method of firefighting. However, with no historical validation, in defense of Crassus' business ethics, which we have already seen as far from admirable, such a scheme attributed to Crassus remains speculative. So, although there must be skepticism that pay-as-you-go firefighting programs originated with Crassus, such programs clearly did not die with him.

As recently as 2010, MSNBC reported that firefighters in Obion County, Tennessee, allowed a home to burn to the ground (figure 3.7) because the homeowner failed to pay a $75 annual firefighter fee. MSNBC's Keith Olbermann aired the story, and the Internet lit up with many bloggers referring to Crassus' "invention" of the idea.

This blot on Crassus' reputation will be more difficult to eradicate than the firefighting fee policy. For after the uproar, the now-renamed "pay-to-spray" policy the South Fulton Fire Department used to support surrounding county residents was changed only two years later so such situations would not be repeated. However, the homeowner would then be charged a fee of $3,500 for putting out the fire (as reported on March 30, 2012, by WBBJ TV on their website www.wbbjtc.com). Some bad ideas are almost as long lived as Crassus' disreputable reputation.

Figure 3.7. A house owned by Gene Cranick of Obion County that burned to the ground as firefighters watched because he had not paid an annual firefighting fee of $75 to the county. (Source: Adam J. Rose, The Huffington Post, 10/05/10.)

Crassus' Workforce—The Architects

Let's examine the concept of creating the brigade and then using it for profit. Plutarch said Crassus "bought slaves, who were architects and builders," but gives no further details. However, there was an interesting exchange of letters between the Emperor Trajan (figure 3.8) and his imperial envoy to ancient Bithynia (modern Turkey) between 110 and 112/3 that sheds light on the rarity of trained architects. The envoy corresponding with Trajan was Pliny the Younger whom we saw earlier complained to Trajan that there were no siphones in Nicomedia.

Figure 3.8. Marble bust of the Emperor Trajan, who in AD 111 declined to provide even one architect to his Bithynian envoy Pliny the Younger.

Over a few letters, Pliny repeatedly requests that the Emperor send just one architect from Rome to him in Bithynia. Satisfying such a request required travel of more than one thousand miles. Trajan, after ignoring the request, responded, "You cannot lack architects: every province has skilled men trained for this work. It is a mistake to think they can be sent out more quickly from Rome when they usually come to us from Greece" (Pliny, *Letters* X.40). Qualified architects in his province must have been very scarce for the fastidious Pliny. So, within Crassus' contingent of more than five hundred slaves, there were likely few architects, perhaps a handful at most, with the balance most likely construction workers.

Crassus had an advantage over Pliny by living in Rome where he could purchase Greek slaves with the specific talent he needed when he wanted, or at least when they were available. As Crassus embarked on his plan to buy endangered tenements, he likely paid the then current market price for the slave talent he needed. (For a discussion of the horrors of Roman slavery, see appendixes C, D, and E) Regardless of how and when Crassus acquired his slave architects, we can draw a key lesson in modern resource management from Crassus acquiring his workforce.

Lesson 7. Obtain the Best Talent Available

For any venture, the entrepreneur, hiring manager, or executive should always seek to hire *and keep* the best people available. To intentionally shortchange any venture by cutting corners in employee quality is to risk the enterprise, for an organization is its people. Crassus likely selected his most critically skilled resources himself, because Plutarch tells his readers early that Crassus "superintended" his slaves' education. If he spent time in their training, it would be reasonable for him to have also spent time in acquiring them. This activity would not have been unique to Crassus. We also know Trajan's imperial envoy, Pliny the Younger, wrote to a relative about his selecting slaves: "I think the slaves you advised me to buy look all right" (Pliny, *Letters* 1.21).

Crassus' Workforce—The Builders

Most of Crassus' workforce was not as specialized as the architects were, so we must assume that the construction workers in a workforce of about five hundred required significant oversight (selection, direction, and deployment). Crassus would likely have expected some men in his construction crews to be well trained to use complex construction devices such as cranes for lifting heavy material at building sites (figure 3.9).

Members of Crassus' construction brigade possibly needed to be trained to use a *ballista* (a traditional Roman military weapon that was a cross between a large bow and a catapult (figure 3.10) to help knock down or deconstruct the "tottering walls" of damaged buildings (Reynolds 1996, 83).[15] Emperor Augustus' fire brigades had ballistae, but the details of the use of such a "weapon" during and/or after the fire remains unclear (Reynolds 1996, 83, 94, 97).[16]

Figure 3.9. A modern rendering of an ancient,
human powered Roman treadwheel crane.
(Image courtesy of TurboSquid.)

Figure 3.10. A modern reconstruction of a small ballista possibly used in a nonmilitary capacity by construction crews to knock down damaged buildings.
(Photo courtesy of Oren Rosen, Wikipedia,
http://upload.wikimedia.org/wikipedia/commons
/6/60/Hecht_090710_Ballista.jpg.)

Last, we might also expect to see Crassus concerned with his brigades' overall ability to follow instructions during the stress of a fire or building collapse—perhaps, like a military force during battle. Crassus would have gained this experience firsthand from his military experience with his father, with Sulla, and in command during Spartacus' slave rebellion.

Crassus' Management Experience

Because Plutarch tells us nothing of Crassus' business management style, we must extrapolate it from what Plutarch says about Crassus' military management skills, based on the assumption that Crassus' command of soldiers (citizens) should be a best-case model for his command of a construction brigade (slaves).

Plutarch reports that in 71 BC, during the slave war, the Roman Senate asked Crassus to lead the Republic's legions after they suffered a number of defeats by Spartacus and his forces. (Spartacus is discussed at length in chapter 5.)

Plutarch also tells us that, after an initial battle in which Spartacus defeated some of Crassus' forces, Crassus identified five hundred soldiers who showed the greatest cowardice in the face of the enemy. He then had the men sorted into fifty groups of ten. From each group of ten, Crassus "took one man, by lot, and put him to death (by clubbing at the hands of their nine comrades-in-arms); thus, inflicting on the soldiers this ancient mode of punishment which had long fallen into disuse" (Plutarch, *Crassus* 10). Crassus had this archaic and brutal punishment of *decimation* carried out in front of the entire army and then marched his legion back into battle against Spartacus. Crassus wanted his soldiers to fear him more than they feared Spartacus—and they did.

Crassus' Management Style

What can we surmise about Crassus' management of his construction brigade from his brutal military example of decimation? The Roman legions had not experienced decimation in more than a century, and they learned their lesson well—they gave Crassus his victory over Spartacus. We can assume, even though the decimation event was a few years away, that Crassus probably demanded that his construction brigade operate to a standard of military precision with which he was familiar from his civil war days and that he was not one to tolerate insubordination or dereliction of duty.

We can also assume that Crassus organized his slave workforce like a traditional Roman military force called a *cohort*. A military cohort consisted of 480 men divided into 6 centuries of 80 legionaries led by a *centurion*, who was helped by a second-in-command and a standard-bearer. If we apply that model, then

Crassus' construction brigade possibly consisted of 6 centuries of 80 builders, a century leader, assistant century leader, and one architect per century, accounting for a workforce of 498 ((80 + 3) x 6 centuries).

If there was also an overall commander of the workforce who had a few slave assistants, we reach Plutarch's stated number of "more than five hundred" slaves. This is pure supposition, but the military analogy fits well because Plutarch referred to Crassus' workforce as a brigade, and we know Augustus also adopted a military structure for freedmen who comprised his firefighting force a few decades later.

Management Span of Control

A century with two "supervisors" produces a span of control of 1 to 40, a large but reasonable manager-to-staff ratio in the services space where workers are near one another (rather than spread all over the city). As a modern example, the ratio of New York City's supervisors to EMTs (Emergency Medical Technicians) in 2014, despite all the available command and control technology, was 1:19 (NYC City Council 2014, 4).[17] A tradeoff must always be made between supervision cost and span of control. Wider spans have less costly management overhead but less supervisory effectiveness, whereas smaller spans facilitate more effective management and control but also incur greater costs.

Crassus' likely application of his military experience to operate his workforce in acquiring multiple properties forms our next entrepreneurial thinking lesson:

Lesson 8. Leverage Your Past

Crassus' use of his experience with the military likely did not stop with the structure he imposed on his workforce. It is difficult to imagine that Crassus dashed around Rome by day (when the streets were most crowded and wheeled travel restricted) or night (in the unlit ancient metropolis) with his brigade in tow at every report of a fire or collapse as he attempted to acquire property.

Most likely, Crassus had agents or subordinates in sections of the city, not unlike scouts in the military, who reported on fires or other calamities and who, perhaps, could even conduct business (the purchase) on his behalf. Taking into account travel time of runners with messages and the brigade's time required to reach a site, by the time any purchase could be executed, the likelihood of a wooden structure surviving a fire was small, and the likelihood of the fire spreading was great. This is most likely the reason Emperor Augustus, a few decades later, found it necessary to permanently distribute and house a much larger firefighting force around the city.

Crassus is not alone in leveraging his experience. Modern research based on data obtained from company founders on *Inc.*'s 1989 list of the one hundred fastest-growing private companies in the US revealed that a significant majority (71 percent) of entrepreneurs obtained their new business ideas from their employment experiences (figure 3.11)(Bhide 1994, 151).[18]

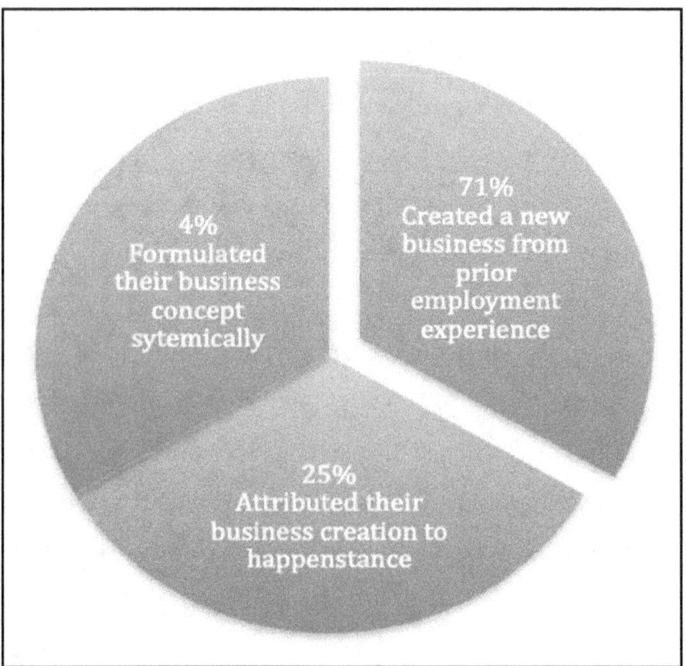

Figure 3.11. Sources for entrepreneurial idea generation based on interviews with founders of *Inc.*'s 1989 list of fastest-growing private companies in the US. (Source: Bhide, 1994, p. 151.)

Crassus' Focus

Once a tenement building was in flames (and likely lost), the risk to nearby buildings threatened, but not yet engulfed, provided the greatest opportunity for Crassus and his agents to rapidly negotiate and consummate several purchases. In such dire circumstances, we can assume Crassus rejected the pay-or-pray approach because Plutarch reported, "the greatest part of Rome fell into the hands of Crassus" (Plutarch, *Crassus* 3).

Crassus' command of Roman property would not have occurred if Crassus accepted a firefighting service fee instead of a property purchase. For if by paying a fee, distressed sellers could preserve their investment, they would have lost their fear of complete ruin, and that fear impelled their sale to Crassus and created the opportunity for Crassus, who had a unique talent for preying on others' misfortunes. Crassus acquired many of Rome's tenements (Plutarch, *Crassus* 2), and despite the ugliness, this chapter's last lesson in entrepreneurial thinking is founded on his unwavering focus on the acquisition of properties at risk.

Lesson 9. Stay Committed to Your Vision

We can assume that Crassus, for conflagrations, recognized he was in the business of buying property, not offering firefighting services for a fee. Crassus likely learned from his military days to stay focused on his core objectives and, as a result, was extraordinarily successful in his ruthless pursuit of an ever-enlarging real estate portfolio.

The Extent of Crassus' Real Estate Business

Plutarch reported that most of Rome's real estate came under Crassus' ownership. We might wonder, though, whether holding great tracts of tenement housing for the poor was the best short-term investment for Crassus, for the property, regardless of ownership, remained vulnerable to destruction. Given that Crassus still worked to rapidly accumulate his wealth, a buy-and-hold strategy would seem less productive than buy and sell. Not that great slumlords have not generated significant wealth over time (and great notoriety), but for the wealth-hungry Crassus, it might have made more sense for him to acquire, repair or rebuild, and then quickly sell the restored property, or in modern parlance, "flip" the property (Ward 1977, 73).[19]

Precedence for Property Flipping in Rome

Crassus was innovative, but it seems he also did not shy from emulating someone else's successful business concept. One real estate speculator during the Late Republic, C. Sergius Orata, refurbished and sold property to the wealthy (Maximus, *Memorable*

Doings and Sayings 9.1). In one particular transaction, Orata failed to disclose an encumbrance to a buyer (some things never change). He was sued and then defended in court by a relative of Crassus (Ward 1977, 73).[20] So, we see that Crassus was likely familiar with the case and the profit potential of flipping high-end properties, of which we have seen there were only about 1,800.

Crassus might easily have extended a version of the business model to the much larger and more vulnerable market of 47,000 tenements. It would therefore not be surprising if Crassus, in buying and selling property, owned much of the property in Rome, but perhaps not all at the same time. Still, we can assume that Crassus was Rome's largest and most successful real estate magnate.

Crassus and the Outsourcing of His Slaves' Services

Crassus' possibly did not use his workforce of more than five hundred exclusively and fully on work associated with property he acquired during catastrophes. A simple answer to any available slack time might be that when not engaged in rebuilding newly acquired dwellings, the brigade worked on Crassus' homes and maintained structures already acquired and rebuilt. However, assuming the tenements were rented, we can expect that Crassus was as proactive in fixing the occupied buildings as a modern slumlord might be. If Crassus had any similarity to his modern counterparts, he did as little as possible, unless ancient landlords were more sensitive to their tenants' needs than modern ones are—not likely.

We have some additional information regarding the former option of working on Crassus' homes. Plutarch reports "though he (Crassus) had so many artisans, he built no house except his own; for he used to say that those who were fond of building were ruined by themselves, without the aid of any opponent" (Plutarch, *Crassus* 2). Here, Plutarch provides a direct quote from Crassus. We see a tightfisted Crassus, whom we can assume was uninterested in having his workforce "ruin" him by expanding his personal residence or building additional ones for his use—so much for a "simple" answer to Crassus' use of the brigade.

Additional Use of Crassus' Construction Brigade

Assuming there was slack time, Crassus undoubtedly did not tolerate his talented slave resources being nonproductive and sitting idle, anticipating the next fire or building collapse. But if they were not working on Crassus' properties, where else could they work? An answer is that the workers were kept busy if Crassus offered his workforce's services to *other* aristocrats for repairs or on their new construction projects for a fee. (Crassus likely was more than helpful if a fellow noble sought to ruin himself by constructing a larger or new residence.) This service would in no way conflict with the property acquisition business, as it used the same skilled resources *when they were available.*

We cannot be certain whether Crassus contracted his slave workforce of architects and builders to others, but Plutarch again provides an interesting bit of information when discussing Crassus' wealth. Plutarch indicates that even though Crassus had numerous silver mines and valuable country estates, his greatest profit came from the value of his talented slaves, including "readers, clerks, assayers of silver, house-managers, and table-servants" (Plutarch, *Crassus* 3).

Ward, in his biography of Crassus, believes Crassus was not keeping such talented slaves solely for his use, but "discovered the principle behind modern manpower rental services. If someone needed the temporary services of a reader or a copyist, Crassus, for a fee, could fill the need from the ranks of his trained slaves. If someone were giving an unusually large banquet, Crassus was right there with necessary extra personnel" (Ward 1977, 73–74).[21]

It is not radical to assume the same applied to the construction brigade, as it fit with the model of providing contract services for a fee, as seen with Crassus' other highly skilled slaves. Regardless of whether the construction brigade's services were included in the large-scale creation and operation of a resource for hire, Crassus again showed that he was an energetic and innovative entrepreneur.

A Supporting Example

Individual slaves were commonly made available to fellow nobles for a specific purpose. For example, Cicero requested that his good friend *and* publisher, Titus Pomponius Atticus, provide him with slaves who could bind, label, and help organize his manuscripts (Cicero, *Atticus* 78; Byrne 1920, 15).[22] Whether the specific services for Cicero were free is unclear, but such services by Atticus were generally provided for profit (Byrne 1920, 14).[23]

Figure 3.12. A fourth-century relief depicting a slave holding his master's writing tablets. (Photo by Giovanni Dall'Orto.)

Therefore, it is not unreasonable to assume that Crassus, the hard-nosed businessman who was unlikely embarrassed to charge a friend a fee, did the same with his construction brigade as he did with his readers, clerks, assayers, house managers, and table servants—he charged for their services.

The slave workforce had no option but to do as Crassus or his agents commanded, as the threat of violence was always present. Slavery, brutal in any modern period, was no less so in ancient Rome (figure 3.13), where slaves had no legal rights or legal standing. Even to testify in court, slaves had to first be tortured, because it was believed they would always lie to protect their masters (who had life and death control over their bodies, as well the ability to free or execute their slaves).

Slavery was an institution that long outlived the Roman Republic. It was not even formally outlawed in the United States until 1865, more than 1,900 years after the death of Crassus and his slave-based business. (See appendixes B, C, D, and E for more detailed descriptions of the horror of Roman slavery.)

Chapter Conclusion

In this chapter, we studied Crassus' approach to the calamities that befell Rome's congested, urban residents and the tottering structures in which they lived. Crassus recognized that buying, repairing, and selling buildings that were damaged or susceptible to damage generated significant profit opportunities. To capitalize on those opportunities, Crassus applied the resources available (slaves) and negotiated from a position of strength.

Figure 3.13. A Roman slave market painted in 1867 by Jean-Leon Gerome.

Where others failed to act, Crassus created a successful business model and added to his wealth by outsourcing talented slaves, which likely included his construction resources when they were not fully engaged in his repairs. The following are four modern lessons that emerged from Crassus' opportunism:

Lesson 6. One Man's Problem Is Another's Business Opportunity

Lesson 7. Obtain the Best Talent Available

Lesson 8. Leverage Your Past

Lesson 9. Stay Committed to Your Vision

The one unmistakable attribute of entrepreneurial thinking that repeatedly appears in Crassus' actions and is at the core of the chapter's four lessons is Crassus' exploitation of opportunities for profit:

Opportunism

Crassus demonstrated an innate inability to repeatedly capitalize on others' misfortunes and needs.

The Robber Baron Attitude

Crassus' ability to see a profit opportunity in others' problems would have sat well with the robber barons, as exemplified by the great banker J. P. Morgan's actions while he was still in his early twenties. During the American Civil War, Morgan allegedly financed a deal (the Hall Carbine Affair) to buy and resell defective rifles purchased from the Army for $3.50. The defective firearms were "retrofitted" to military standards and resold back to a desperate Union Army for $22 each. It turned out that Northern soldiers were likely to lose a thumb when firing the retrofitted guns (Josephson 1995, 61).[24]

As with the early tales of Crassus' wealth accumulation, it is difficult to distinguish between fact and folklore in determining Morgan's knowledge of the details of this despicable deal, but Morgan, like Crassus, learned early that desperation is the handmaiden of great profit. That realization helped propel Morgan and many other robber barons of the Gilded Age to great wealth, just as Crassus was propelled to great wealth in the ancient Roman Republic. The robber barons' disregard for the welfare of their workers (and their families) was caricatured in an 1883 Puck cartoon (figure 3.14).

Figure 3.14. Robber barons protected from hard times by sandbags full of their money on a raft carried on the backs of the working poor. (Puck 7 February 1883. Courtesy Library of Congress, Print & Photographic Division.)

Chapter 4. Crassus and Financial Services

Crassus and Credit Services

The next business of Crassus that we will study provides further insight into both Crassus' entrepreneurial thinking and his vision. Plutarch informs us that Crassus "used to lend money to his friends without interest; but he would demand it back immediately on the expiration of the time of the borrower, which made the gratuitous loan more burdensome than heavy interest" (Plutarch, *Crassus* 3).

We must understand that Crassus acted in a fashion that more resembles modern mortgage and investment bankers than the ancient moneychangers made famous by Jesus' casting them out (figure 4.1) in his effort to cleanse the Temple in Jerusalem (John 2:13–16; Matt. 21:12–13). The moneychangers of the Gospels were converting (at a profit) Roman and Greek coinage into coin acceptable in the Temple where supplicants then purchased a sacrificial animal. Crassus, like many of his senatorial colleagues, was at the other end of the banking spectrum, financing the needs of powerful "friends" and, possibly, provincial rulers of client states or cities with interest, of course.

Figure 4.1. A nineteenth-century painting by Carl Bloch of Jesus casting out the moneychangers from the Temple in Jerusalem.

Cicero, our frequent source on the morals of ancient businessmen, had nothing good to say about bankers if they charged clients high interest rates (it was unbecoming a gentlemen to be usurious), but we cannot determine from Plutarch or Cicero himself whether Crassus fell into this category with his interest-paying clients. Despite this interest rate uncertainty, let's look at the implications of both elements of Crassus' credit operation: first, the interest-bearing loans and second, Crassus' loans to friends.

The Example of Atticus

In the last chapter, we saw that Atticus provided literary services through lending his talented slaves to Cicero. Atticus was a close friend of Cicero despite Atticus' occupation as a financier to the elite, and for our purposes here, a banker. Atticus operated in the same period as Crassus, and they may well have done business together. Atticus was also associated with Caesar, with Pompey the Great, and even with Sulla.

In fact, Atticus was well acquainted with Sulla, for during the Sullan civil war, Atticus exiled himself to Athens, as Crassus had to Spain, and while in Athens, Atticus spent time with Sulla before Sulla's march on Rome. Sulla was so taken with Atticus that he requested Atticus join him, but Atticus declined the offer (and survived to tell of it).

We know much about Atticus' banking activities because Cornelius Nepos' biography of him has survived from antiquity. (For much more detail on Atticus' life and career, see *Career Turbulence: Ancient Lessons for Survival in the Modern Workplace* by this author).[1] Nepos tells us that Atticus not only provided loans to aristocrats, but also to cities such as Athens. I present these loans as examples of interest-bearing loans that might have been typical of the loans Crassus made.

Atticus and Athens

We learn from Atticus' dealings with the Athenians that "he never exacted from them excessive interest, nor would he allow them to remain in debt beyond the stipulated time" (Nepos, *Atticus* 2.4). Thus, we see interest was charged (perhaps at 12 percent a year), and the Athenians were expected to repay the loan fully and on schedule. Nepos considers the demand for timely loan repayments a virtue, whereas Crassus' biographer (Plutarch) sees the same demand as a vice, labeling the practice as "burdensome."

Atticus and Sicyon

What if a client failed to repay a loan? In Cicero's letters to him, we see a frustrated Atticus in 61, 60, and 59 BC, repeatedly seeking Cicero's help in forcing the repayment of a debt owed him by the ancient Greek city of Sicyon. Pliny the Younger's uncle (Pliny the Elder) reported that in 56 BC all of Sicyon's native paintings were "sold to meet a debt of the community, and were removed from ownership of the state to Rome" (Pliny, *Natural History* XXXV.XL.127). We have no definitive information that the creditor was Atticus, but the result is clear—a debt of the city was repaid through the coerced sale of the city's art collection.

The Athenians, unlike Sicyon, paid their debts on time and viewed Atticus as a fair lender, so we might expect Crassus to have offered interest rates and terms similar to those of Atticus. On the other hand, Crassus made a fortune from doing business with those most in need, so he may have charged a premium rate for his loans. However, Plutarch never says Crassus was usurious; he only indicates that Crassus unfailingly demanded payments as committed from his clients.

Why Crassus' "Friends" Required Loans

A significant amount of Rome's real estate, and possibly many in the Roman Senate, came under Crassus' control. Ancient Roman senators, because so much of their wealth was tied up in great estates, were land rich and cash poor. As aristocrats climbed the career ladder hoping to gain the highest office—the consulship— they were required to spend huge amounts of money to obtain the public's adulation with gladiatorial games, gifts such as food or cash, or the construction of public buildings for use by Rome's citizens.

An Example of the Cost of Winning the People's Adulation

Perhaps, the best example of the cost of winning public support in the Late Republic comes from Crassus' political adversary, Pompey the Great. Pompey had no need for Crassus' financial services, as he was extraordinarily wealthy, but to win public admiration beyond what his military successes engendered, Pompey constructed the first permanent theater in Rome (figure 4.2).

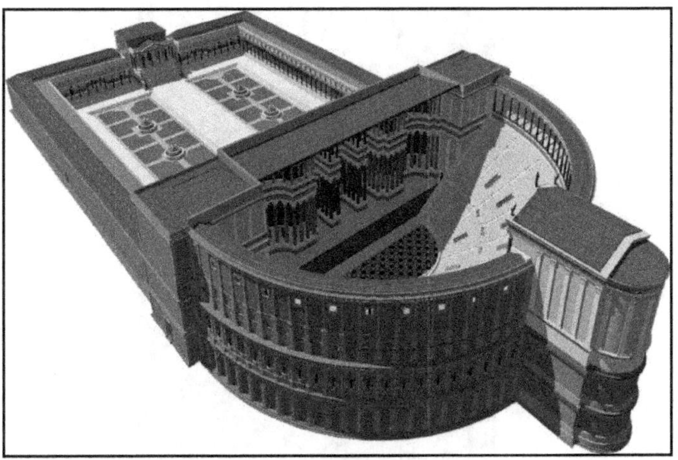

Figure 4.2. A model of Pompey's theater and its surrounding structures, including at the far right at the top row of the seats/stairs, a Temple to Venus Victrix (Venus the Victorious). The park on the left, known as Pompey's portico, included halls for meetings, fountains, gardens, statuary and Pompey's art collection.

"No one had ever before been permitted to build a permanent theater in Rome; it was considered a decadent luxury. To satisfy social mores, a Temple of Venus Victrix was built at the center of the top row of seats; the vast seating space thus served as a

glorified staircase to the temple" (Stambaugh 1988, 42–43).[2]
Pompey was determined to have his theater and win the people's
adulation for its construction. The theater complex, which likely
also included a statue of himself (figure 4.3) prominently displayed
in the public meetinghouse, took six years to complete.

Figure 4.3. Statue of Crassus' frequent adversary and
occasional partner, Pompey the Great, which once
may have stood in Pompey's theater complex.

The dedication of the structure coincided with Pompey's
second term as consul, serving with Crassus in 55 BC. Cicero, in a
letter to Atticus, tells us that Atticus helped Pompey with the
theater's display of Pompey's art (Cicero, *Atticus* 85.1).

Why Crassus Offered Loans to Friends

Crassus' friends, as Plutarch mentioned, were eligible for interest-free loans from Crassus, but he still demanded repayment as promised, which Plutarch says was even "more burdensome than heavy interest." Why would Crassus offer interest-free loans if he were trying to increase his wealth? The answer is that these loans were not to make money, but to obtain political support. Crassus well knew other senators could be manipulated if they were in debt to him, and thus, Crassus could use his wealth to obtain greater power in Rome. Crassus was known to demand repayment of the loan "immediately on the expiration of the time," forcing the borrower to pay up, or perhaps be forced to settle another way—supporting Crassus in whatever political agenda he followed. From this approach to exchanging financial capital for political leverage, we form our final lesson in entrepreneurial thinking from Crassus.

Lesson 10. A Friend in Need Is a Friend Indeed

This lesson is not intended as a tutorial in acquiring political power, rather a lesson in obtaining and maintaining leverage. When negotiating any business transaction, you should be as opportunistic as Crassus was, know your goals, and then work to understand both what a potential partner wants most as well as the availability of any competitive offerings.

One of those friends receiving perhaps the greatest credit Crassus ever extended to one person was Julius Caesar as he prepared to leave Rome for the governorship of Spain in 62 BC. Plutarch and other ancient historians, such as Suetonius in his biography of Caesar (Suetonius, *Caesar* 9) as well as Caesar himself (Caesar *Civil War*, 3.16.3) documented Caesar's significant debt at the time of his departure. So, Crassus' role in the story is irrefutable. Plutarch reports the following:

> *When Caesar was going to Iberia (Spain), as praetor (governor), and had no money in consequence of his creditors having come upon him and seizing all his outfit (his baggage, not unlike Sicyon's art), Crassus did not leave him in this difficulty, but got him released, by becoming security (i.e. surety) for him to the amount of eight hundred and thirty talents* (Plutarch, *Crassus* 7).

To compete with the likes of Pompey and Crassus in acquiring public and senatorial support, Caesar needed to spend a phenomenal amount of money he did not have, and so we see that Caesar, a popular politician (and the future dictator), was in

Crassus' debt and would remain deeply in debt if he failed to repay his creditors the 830 talents of gold owed (nearly $1.6 billion today).

Crassus and Ancient Tax Collectors

Although Crassus was not a moneychanger of the ilk Jesus so despised, he was linked to another detested class of biblical moneymen—the tax collectors, known as *publicans*, who were hated by the ancient Judeans as well as most other provincials. This is seen repeatedly in the New Testament where Jesus singles out publicans as sinners, but also declares that they can still find salvation (Luke 18:10–14, 19:2–8). And in Matthew 9:9–12 (figure 4.4), we find the story of Jesus and His calling of Saint Matthew:

Jesus saw a man named Matthew, sitting in the customhouse. And He said unto him, "Follow Me." And he arose and followed Him. And it came to pass as Jesus sat at a meal in the house, behold, many publicans and sinners came and sat down with Him and His disciples. And when the Pharisees saw it, they said unto His disciples, "Why eateth your master with publicans and sinners?"

Figure 4.4. A 1616 painting by Hendrick Terbruggen of Jesus calling Saint Matthew the publican in Matthew 9.9–12.

These biblical depictions of the publicans have forever linked the hated ancient tax collectors of antiquity with sinners. So, why spend any ink on discussing these ancient sinners? It turns out that during the Roman Republic, these "sinners" were employed by private companies, and these *for-profit* companies collected taxes for the state. And where profit intersected with government, we find Crassus' tight-fisted hand.

The Tax-Collecting Companies and the Roman Senate

Crassus' link to the despised publicans was so remote, and perhaps intentionally hidden, that Plutarch didn't mention it. We must look to Cicero's letters to piece together Crassus' relationship with the publicans. The large tax-collecting companies that employed the local publicans described in the Bible were privately owned, for-profit companies that obtained multiyear rights to collect taxes and tolls from the Roman Senate through contracts let and overseen by former Roman consuls called *censors*. These companies' profits came from wrenching additional monies from the provincials *beyond the contract bid amount* —hence the hatred.

The Asian Tax-Collection Contracts

To understand Crassus' involvement with the publicans, we must again look to Cicero and his letters to Atticus. In 61 BC, a number of the tax-collecting "companies which had contracted with the censors for Asia (today part of Turkey and Greece) (figure 4.5) complained that in the heat of the competition, they had taken the contract at an excessive price; they demanded that the contract should be annulled" (Cicero, *Atticus*, 1.17.9). Cicero informed Atticus in 61 BC that tax contracts were let to collect taxes across all Roman Asia, but because of aggressive competition, the contracted price was bid so high that the companies that won the bid faced significant financial losses.

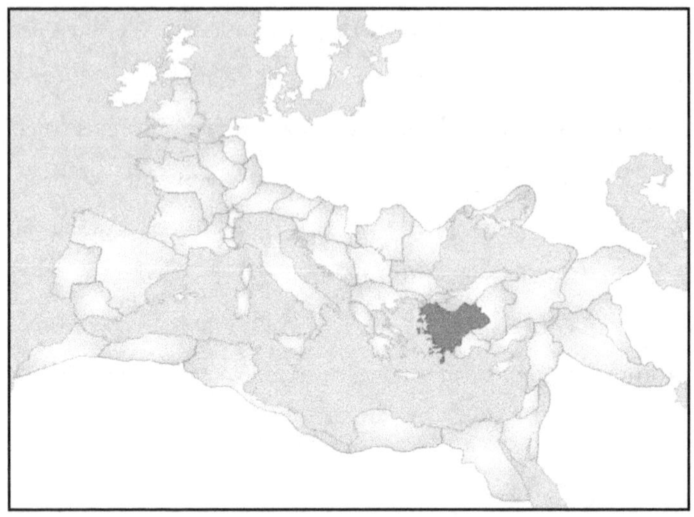

Figure 4.5. Map showing the ancient Roman province of Asia (now part of modern Turkey and Greece) where, in 61 BC, publicans overbid for the right to collect taxes (area in dark grey).

These five-year Asian contracts comprised a "significant" portion of an estimated $800 million in the Roman Republic's annual public revenues (Badian 1983, 63).[3] As a result, the winning bidders asked the Senate to cancel the contracts. Cicero informed his friend that he led support in the Senate for the annulment of the contracts, but then Cicero corrected himself: "I led in their support, or rather, I was second, for it was Crassus who induced them to venture on this demand" (Cicero, *Atticus* 1.17.9). Thus, we have Cicero telling Atticus that the tax-collecting companies made their request only after Crassus "induced" them to do so.

Perhaps, Crassus stayed closer to his principles, however questionable, than Cicero did, for Cicero wrote that you should reject a livelihood from collecting taxes as it "incurs people's ill-will" (Cicero, *On Duties* XLII.150). Crassus at this point was one of the most powerful men in Rome. So, why did Crassus take public actions for the tax collectors and their companies? The likely answer here is unsurprising—profit, or in this instance, the absence thereof.

Crassus and the Asian Tax Collectors

Powerful men in Rome, including Julius Caesar, (Maximus, *Memorable Doings and Sayings* vi. 9) often bought and sold shares in the large tax-collecting companies, despite the aristocratic disdain. Crassus' vigorous effort for the Asian publicans suggests that he was a large shareholder in the Asia tax-collecting corporation (Badian 1983, 103).[4] If the company had losses or went bankrupt, Crassus suffered a significant personal loss—hence, his keen interest in fixing the problem of the Asian publicans overbidding and under collecting.

Crassus and Cicero (whose friend Atticus was also a large supporter of the tax-collecting companies) failed to gain the annulment of the tax contracts in the Senate, for such an effort had not been tried for more than 125 years (it lost then too). However, in 60 BC, with Crassus' backing, Julius Caesar was elected consul for the first time, and within a few months in office, Caesar forced through a tax quota reduction in Asia, reducing what the publicans owed by one-third (Suetonius, *Julius Caesar* 20). Crassus, after failing to win passage of the bill he wanted in the Senate, needed Caesar in power to achieve his goal (or goals), and Caesar, likely still in Crassus' debt, needed Crassus and his support to win his election. A friend in need truly is a friend indeed.

Modern Publicans

Before we unduly chastise Crassus for his role with the hated publicans, let's take a moment to understand that "for-profit" collection of taxes is not as alien to our modern society as we might first think. As recently as 2015 the US Congress has allowed the Internal Revenue Service to enter into contracts with private debt-collection companies to collect Federal income taxes owed. These private companies earn a commission of up to 25 percent of the money they recover, and in 2019 they collected over $200M. So, as in the cases of "pay to spray" and influence buying, we again see an ugly ancient activity for which Crassus has been harshly criticized successfully worm its way into modern statecraft.

Chapter Conclusion

In this chapter, we studied Crassus' provision of financial services, which, like his real estate transactions and his outsourcing businesses, targeted his wealthy friends, other aristocratic associates, and possibly provincial governments. We also established that Crassus had links to the provincial tax collectors and the reasons he preferred to operate behind the scenes, for such influence as his often yields its greatest dividends in the shadows. Whether in hidden recesses (his loans to senators and his relations with the publicans) or exposed to public scrutiny (the backstopping of Caesar's loans from his creditors), Crassus, as his peers, traded credit for influence with all willing to deal, and in his case, there were many. Crassus demonstrated the timelessness of the adage that formed this chapter's sole lesson from him.

Lesson 10. A Friend in Need Is a Friend Indeed

The following attributes of entrepreneurial thinking underpin this lesson from the mature Crassus:

Vision

Crassus, by focusing his wealth on achieving his vision, gained

political influence and power, either directly or through others
indebted to him through his judiciously made loans.

Tenacity

Crassus, once he deployed his resources, maintained an iron
grip on their terms of repayment, likely demanding political
"favors" to provide funds, both at the time of the loan and
when a debt was at risk of late repayment or default.

The Robber Baron Attitude

America's most famous and successful banker of the Gilded Age, J.
P. Morgan (figure 4.6), was continually approached, as Crassus was,
by those needing money. Morgan provided key insight into his
natural skepticism and the thinking of many powerful men with
whom he dealt: "A man always has two reasons for doing a thing.
One that sounds good, and the real one."

Likely, Crassus would have heartily agreed with Morgan.
We can also assume that Crassus was not focusing on his social
bonds of friendship with his fellow aristocrats when he extended
them credit—nothing personal, but this was business. This same
hard-nosed approach to doing business with friends became
Cornelius Vanderbilt's axiom, for he often said, "There is no

friendship in trade" (Stiles 2010, 223).[5] We can assume there would

be no argument from Crassus on this point.

Figure 4.6. J. P. Morgan as the Pied Piper in a 1902 Joseph Keppler caricature. Following Morgan is a host of characters (likely self-described friends) seeking to do business with the great banker.

Chapter 5. The Rise and Fall of Crassus

Crassus and the Seduction of a Vestal Virgin

Despite Crassus' great wealth, the road to supreme power was not guaranteed, and Crassus was not immune from prosecution for illegal behavior. The events surrounding Crassus' accumulation of wealth discussed in the prior chapters did not result in prosecution for a crime under Roman law, which reinforces the point that Crassus' methods may have been distasteful to his contemporaries, but he probably committed no crime. However, there was an attempted prosecution of Crassus in 73 BC (Ward 1977, 75, n. 57).[1]

This legal case involving Crassus shows the vulnerability to prosecution of even one of the most powerful men in Rome—and his guilt or innocence was less relevant than the political leverage to be gained by his adversaries at public trial. A guilty verdict, at least from his enemies' perspective, would have been even better. The charge involving Crassus and a Vestal Virgin (figure 5.1) provided Plutarch such a salacious opportunity to show the extent of Crassus' acquisitiveness and lust for property that Plutarch inserted the story of Crassus' prosecution into the opening section of his biography.

Figure 5.1. A statue in Rome showing the dress of a vestal virgin. It was always suspect for a private citizen to spend too much time with a vestal.

The following is from Plutarch:

> *He was charged with criminal intercourse with Licinia, one of the vestal virgins, who was brought to trial; the prosecutor was one Plotinus. Licinia had a pleasant estate in the suburbs, which Crassus wished to get at a small price, and with this view he was continually about the woman and paying his court to her, which brought on him the suspicion of a criminal intercourse; but he was acquitted by the judges, being indebted in some degree to his love of money for his acquittal from the charge of debauching the vestal. But he never remitted his attentions to Licinia till he got possession of the property.* (Plutarch, *Crassus* 1)

The Role of the Vestals

The six vestal virgins were priestesses of Vesta, goddess of the hearth and oversaw the maintenance of Rome's sacred fire. The fire symbolized Rome's security and could never go out (figure 5.2). If the eternal fire was extinguished, the Romans believed the goddess ended her protection of the city. In fact, the fire remained lit for more than one thousand years, and it was not extinguished until AD 394 (figure 5.3). The Visigoths then sacked the unprotected "eternal city" in AD 410.

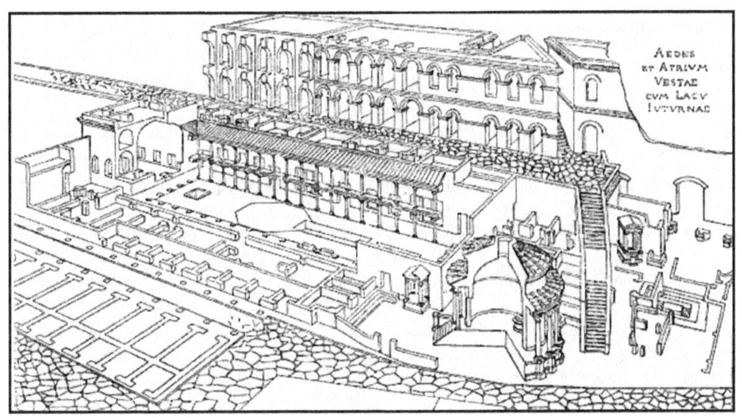

Figure 5.2. A reconstruction of the House of the Vestals. The hearth containing the eternal fire is the circular structure (lower right).

Figure 5.3. The ruins of the Hearth of Vesta still visible in Rome. (Photo by FrankCJones.)

Crassus Only Guilty of Avarice

If a vestal's chastity was violated, the state suffered damage, and the vestal's punishment was to be buried alive. If found guilty, the fate of the man involved was death by scourging "at the hands of the *pontifex maximus* (Rome's chief priest, who at the time was Julius Caesar) or his servants" (Cadoux 2005, 165).[2] Thus, the charges against Licinia and Crassus, which Plutarch says a man named Plotinus brought, were serious.

Plutarch also tells us that Crassus was found innocent because his defense was that he merely wanted the woman's villa. Thus, Crassus was acquitted based on the jury believing he was just plain greedy and not an adulterer. However, the point that Plutarch makes is that Crassus' avarice was in fact so well known in Rome that a jury of senators on the law courts (who might have already been in Crassus' debt or willing to accept a bribe) could easily find him innocent because of his unbridled lust for money.

The Hand of Pompey

In his biography of Crassus, Ward could identify only two Plotinuses alive at the time of Crassus' prosecution, and both had ties to Pompey the Great. Therefore, the charge against Crassus was most likely politically motivated (Ward 1977, 74–75).[3] Plutarch also reports that Crassus got the property he desperately wanted.

Thus, despite the risks, including the social stigma of having his avarice proved to all, Crassus showed amazing passion in his efforts to acquire a property he greatly desired.

Crassus' Passion Was Not Unique

Regardless of the century, entrepreneurs have always been seen as passionate about their business, for if they fail to believe in their idea, how can other potential stakeholders commit their time and resources to the venture? This entrepreneurial passion's importance has been borne out by a recent study of its impact on the investment community (Cardon, Sudek & Mitteness 2009).[4] In this study, 150 angel investors (typically wealthy, early-stage investors) were asked to rate the importance of an entrepreneur's passion on their decision to invest—on a 5-point scale, with 5 being most important. It turns out that entrepreneurial passion was rated at just over 4.5. An entrepreneur's passion matters to the investment community.

Passion, Like Planning, Can Be Overrated

This affirmation of the importance of passion was not unanimous. One investor in the above study remarked, "No amount of passion can make a pig fly" (Cardon, Sudek & Mitteness 2009, 6).[5] This limitation on passion's relevance is echoed on the *Harvard Business*

Review blog network, where Daniel Isenberg, a professor of management practice at Babson College, wrote that entrepreneurs "should leave [their] passion in the bedroom" (Isenberg 2010). These critics of entrepreneurial passion understand its importance, but they also recognize that winning support for a new business concept is challenging, and passion alone does not ensure success.

Plutarch successfully highlights Crassus' passions. Those passions focused on his efforts to gain vengeance, immense wealth, and great political influence—hardly a lofty list of aspirations to be admired and emulated, but the determination and entrepreneurial thinking Crassus showed as he marched along his chosen path is certainly remarkable, if not admirable. Let's now pick up on Crassus' progress as he moved relentlessly toward the pinnacle of power in Rome.

Spartacus' Rebellion

In 73 BC, the same year as Crassus' victory in court, a gladiator named Spartacus escaped from his training school near modern Naples with about seventy men and made his way to Mount Vesuvius to avoid recapture. Spartacus was born in Thrace, an ancient geographic area now apportioned among modern Greece, Bulgaria, and Turkey (figure 5.4).

Figure 5.4. Ancient Thrace, the birthplace of Spartacus, now split among Greece, Bulgaria, and Turkey.

Spartacus, according to various ancient sources, might have been a legionary auxiliary with the Romans, a deserter from the Roman legions, and/or a robber. However, all sources agree that the Roman legions captured and enslaved Spartacus. Because of Spartacus' great courage and strength, he was bought and trained to be a gladiator (figure 5.5).

Figure 5.5. A victorious gladiator in an 1872 painting by Jean-Leon Gerome. The gladiator depicted in this painting appears to have just fought in the Colosseum, which was not completed until nearly a century and a half after Spartacus' death.

Plutarch adds color to the legend of Spartacus by reporting, "When Spartacus was first taken to Rome to be sold, a snake was seen folded over his face while he was sleeping" (Plutarch, *Crassus* 8). The snake portends greatness and/or indicates a link to underworld forces. After his escape, Spartacus and his men were victorious in multiple battles against the forces the Roman Senate dispatched against him. With each successive victory, Spartacus' reputation grew exponentially, as did his army, for thousands of escaped slaves flocked to his side, hoping to win their freedom. By

72 BC, with Spartacus fielding an army of more than seventy thousand warriors, the full-fledged slave insurrection (also known as the Third Servile War) panicked the Roman Senate so much that they turned to Crassus, hoping he would win the war with Spartacus.

Figure 5.6. The larger-than-life marble statue of the gladiator Spartacus sculpted in 1827 by Denis Foyatier and now housed in the Louvre in Paris. The image depicts when Spartacus literally broke his chains of slavery and prepared for his revenge on Rome. (Copyright: pseudolongino/Shutterstock.com.)

Crassus Raises Six Legions

In the period after his victory with Sulla in 82 BC, Crassus amassed a fortune large enough to allow him to personally finance an army of six legions for the fight with Spartacus. This perhaps explains why the Roman Senate selected Crassus, with his limited military experience, for the job, because the state treasury was nearly depleted after years of civil war. Pompey the Great was unavailable to take the command because he was pre-occupied with a war in Spain.

The men Crassus recruited to fight Spartacus were likely Sulla's retired veterans. These would have been combined with any surviving soldiers previously enlisted to battle Spartacus, because most other experienced legions were stationed on Rome's borders (and the Senate reasoned that this was just a battle with rebellious slaves). Although the Senate likely reimbursed Crassus, the cost of maintaining this army in the field for a year has been estimated at 550–600 talents (Ward 1977, 69),[7] over $1.1 billion today. Crassus' business interests had been very profitable indeed.

Crassus Victorious

Crassus' legions must have learned well from the lesson of decimation he impressed on them, for by early 71 BC, they had won the war against Spartacus and his slave army (but not without some timely help from Pompey, who returned victorious from his battles in Spain). His victory in no way softened Crassus. After defeating Spartacus, Crassus ordered the crucifixion of 6,000 of Spartacus' surviving followers, possibly including women and children, as the requisite punishment for their rebellion and as a gruesomely spectacular deterrent to other slaves who might look to follow that rebellious path (Strauss 2009, 190–195).[7]

Figure 5.7. An 1878 painting by Fyodor Andreyevich Bronnikov depicting the crucifixion of 6,000 of Spartacus' soldiers following his defeat by Crassus. Crassus lined the well-travelled Appian Way between Capua, where the revolt began, and Rome, with the crucified victims of the rebellion. "Since the road was 211 kilometers long, anyone traveling between Rome and Capua encountered a crucified slave every thirty-five meters. The spectacle served as a brutal warning of the fate of slave rebels and a memorable display of the futility of rebellion" (Joshel 2010, 63).[8]

Crassus' Ultimate Goal

With his defeat of Spartacus, Crassus won the Roman people's gratitude, especially that of other senators who greatly feared a slave insurrection. After his victory, Crassus remarked, "that no amount of wealth was enough for the man who aspired to be the foremost citizen of the state, unless with the income from it he could maintain an army" (Cicero, *On Duties* I.25). From this statement famous in antiquity, we have Crassus' admission to his ultimate goal. Crassus desired to amass a colossal fortune and then use that fortune to become the "foremost citizen" of Rome.

Crassus and the Public

However, one additional element on the path to becoming Rome's leading citizen still eluded Crassus—winning the Roman people's adulation. The means to attain the requisite glory for becoming Rome's foremost citizen was historically, at least, one great military victory and being awarded a triumph (a grand military procession through Rome's streets (appendix F)) by the Roman Senate to celebrate that victory.

Pompey the Great had already celebrated two triumphs (the first granted by Sulla in 81 or 80 BC and a second in 71 BC). Crassus defeated Spartacus, but his victory's glory was tainted, for Spartacus was not a respected foreign foe, but just a "mere" escaped slave. So, there would be no triumph for Crassus (although there was a lesser celebration called an *ovation*). However, in Crassus' quest to be elected to Rome's highest office, Spartacus' defeat was significant, and he still had all the support his money could buy.

Crassus Elected Consul of Rome

In 70 BC, Crassus was elected consul of Rome. Two consuls were elected annually, and they had supreme authority for the state (figure 5.8). By ascending to the consulship, Crassus reached his goal to gain the Republic's most powerful office, but he had to share the office with the other man Roman citizens elected consul—none other than Pompey the Great. The Senate granted Pompey special exemptions to stand for election—he was too young, not yet a senator, had not held the required offices, was absent from Rome during the campaigning, yet he was there to share supreme power with Crassus.

Pompey, upon returning with his legions from his victories in Spain, defeated a number of escapees from Spartacus' beaten army (Plutarch, *Crassus* 11). Then Pompey, "to diminish the credit due Crassus, claimed credit for ending the war with Spartacus" (Seager 2002, 36).[9]

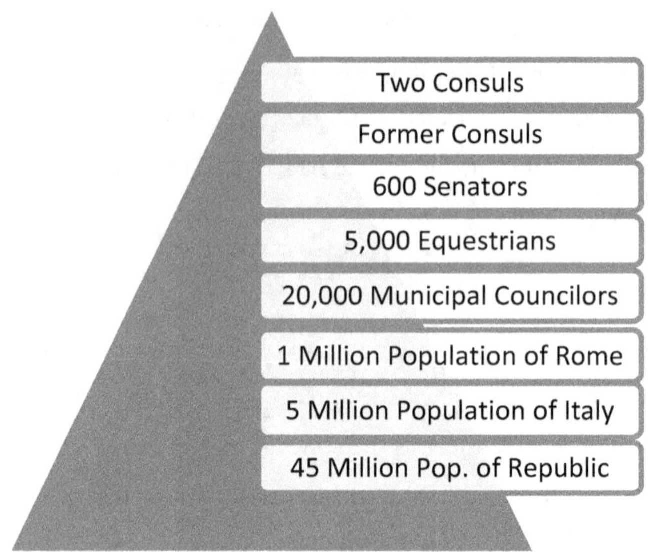

Figure 5.8. Crassus' position as consul in the Late Republic. (Note: The population figures for the equestrians (an upper class of Romans without the money-making constraints of senators, but subordinate to them in status), councilors, and the population of Rome and Italy come from the early years of the Roman Empire, a period shortly after Crassus' death, and an age in which we have more detailed census data).

Pompey's and Caesar's Shadows

Pompey the Great, despite his youth, was his generation's leading general, although another general with greater conquests, nipped at his heels—Julius Caesar, a man still in debt to Crassus. How could Crassus compete with the great victories of his co-consul Pompey, who celebrated his second triumph just before beginning his term as co-consul with Crassus, and Julius Caesar's rising star? Caesar enjoyed great personal favor with the masses, as he spent lavishly to win elective office (recall the size of his debt Crassus guaranteed), served as Pontifex Maximus (an office enthusiastically claimed by Rome's future emperors beginning with Augustus, as shown in Figure 5.9), and was now winning military glory. Crassus had reached the highest elective Roman office, only to be overshadowed by Pompey and Caesar's achievements.

Figure 5.9. Julius Caesar's grandnephew, both emperor and chief priest of the Romans, dressed as the Pontifex Maximus.

Crassus Buys Popularity

With wealth and power only a piece of the leadership puzzle,

Crassus' challenge was how to win additional popularity and distinction. Crassus had no choice but to do so the old-fashioned way—he bought it! Soon after becoming consul with Pompey, Crassus, according to Plutarch (*Crassus* 2), spent a large part of his wealth, for he "dedicated the tenth part of his property to Hercules, and feasted the people (*at 10,000 tables*), and gave every Roman out of his own means enough to maintain him for three months."

Crassus was stubbornly consistent in achieving his goals, despite the cost to his reputation. So, why apply that same steely determination and make such a spectacular display to Hercules now? Crassus could have chosen the dedication for several reasons:

1. Hercules was associated with military victory. This association would remind the people of his victory over Spartacus and, therefore, possibly counterbalance Pompey's recent triumph, for victorious generals traditionally dedicated 10 percent of their booty to Hercules, and Sulla even made an offering of 10 percent of *his entire fortune* (Meier 1982, 130).[10]

2. In earlier Roman times, a 10 percent tithe of commercial profits was dedicated to Hercules, allowing Crassus to display his great wealth to the Roman people.

3. There was also a useful myth that in pre-Roman times,

Hercules defeated the fire-breathing giant Cacus, who terrorized the countryside by devouring human flesh and then nailing his victims' heads to his door (figure 5.10). Perhaps, Crassus not-so subtly reminded his fellow senators of the terror of Spartacus, from which they were now spared.

Figure 5.10. A sixteenth-century engraving by Sebald Beham of Hercules killing a fire-breathing Cacus. This myth may have been useful as a reminder of Crassus' role in defeating Spartacus.

Regardless of the underlying reasons for sacrificing to

Hercules, Crassus, who was so zealous in wealth accretion, was apparently prepared to spend that wealth to achieve his goal of becoming the leading man in Roman politics. But Crassus did not stop there, and his next step showed his true political dexterity.

The Triumvirate

The crafty Crassus followed another adage: If you can't beat them, join them. Both Caesar and Pompey, controlling vast armies of loyal soldiers, now competed. Caesar was already deeply indebted to Crassus and a frequent political ally. Pompey would never yield to Crassus alone, but a full political alliance of Caesar (with his battle-tested legions) and Crassus (with his tremendous wealth) posed great danger to Pompey, the Senate, and the Republic.

Crassus recognized that both Caesar and Pompey would fear him aligning with the other, and that fear could be leveraged. So, in 60 BC, the entrepreneurial Crassus combined forces with both men to control the Roman Senate, magistrate election, and the Republic itself. Plutarch tells us how Crassus pulled off that alliance, known as the *Triumvirate*:

> *When all Rome became divided into three parties—that of Pompeius, Caesar and Crassus; Crassus, by keeping a middle position, used both*

Cicero and the Triumvirate

The three-way marriage of convenience of Crassus, Caesar, and Pompey had fear as its handmaiden. There is no silence here from Cicero's corner, an active participant in, and then victim of, events unleashed.

In 60 BC, Caesar invited Cicero to join Pompey, Crassus, and him in their joint rule, but Cicero declined, for he felt such combination spelled the Republic's doom, and he was correct. In mid-July of 59 BC, Cicero wrote to Atticus:

<blockquote>

Of the political situation, I shall say little. I am terrified by now for fear the very paper may betray us. So henceforward, if I have occasion to write you at any length, I shall obscure my meaning with code terms. As things are, Rome is dying of a strange malady. Disapproval of what has been done and indignant complaint are universal. Opinion is not divided at any point, there is open grumbling, even to the stage of loud groaning, but nobody comes forward with a remedy. This is because we think resistance is bound to be suicidal.. (Cicero, Atticus 2.20.3–4)

</blockquote>

A year later, when the Triumvirate withheld its support from the independent Cicero, long-time political enemies forced Cicero's exile from Rome and burned his house to the ground. This was the same palatial house Cicero was so proud of acquiring earlier from Crassus. In 57 BC, a chastised Cicero returned to Rome, and though now publicly supportive of the triumvirs, the always outspoken Cicero chose to quietly focus on his philosophical writings, and not the violent politics of the day.

Only after Caesar's assassination in 44 BC did Cicero fully return to public politics but with the result that he was proscribed by a new generation of strongmen (the Second Triumvirate), who followed the well-trod path of Caesar, Pompey, and Crassus.

Crassus Seeks a War with Parthia

Ultimately, Crassus must have been dissatisfied with his position in the Triumvirate. For as the second consulship for Crassus and Pompey ended in 55 BC, Caesar kept control of his soldiers and his war in Gaul. Pompey was given Spain to govern from Rome and Crassus sought and received control of the province of Syria (figure 5.11).

Historians have felt that Crassus sought this assignment so he could wage war against the neighboring empire of Parthia (figure 5.12). Syria would provide Crassus an opportunity to burnish his military résumé to keep up with Caesar's continuing successes and to close the gap with Pompey's past successes.

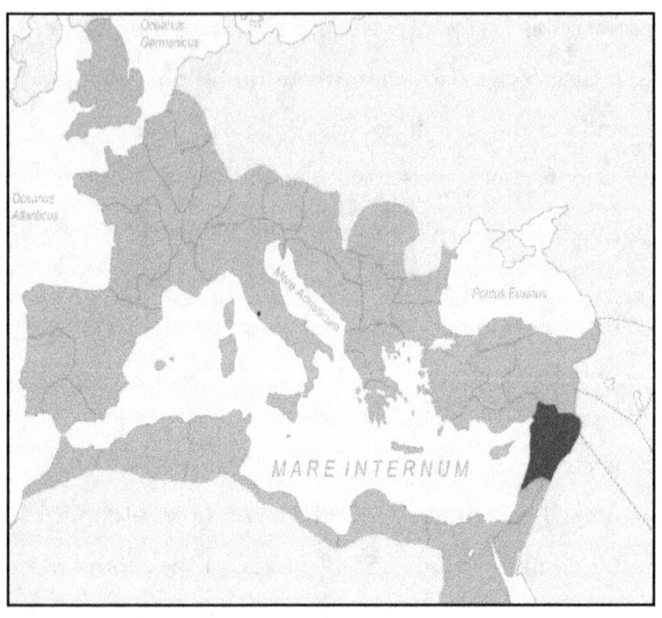

Figure 5.11. Map showing the Syrian Province (far right in dark grey) in a geographic map of the Roman Empire in AD 116. (Map courtesy of ThomasPusch, http://en.wikipedia.org/wiki/File:Syria_SPQR.png.)

Crassus was now more than 60 years old, and he had not fought in battle for at least fifteen years. Yet, he still looked to compete with his younger fellow triumvirs in military glory, especially with his 47-year-old, former protégé, Julius Caesar. Caesar and his legions fought almost continuously for nearly a decade and twice invaded Britain (in 55 BC and 54 BC). Caesar also published his dispatches (*The Gallic War*) to the Senate on the battles he fought, to great acclaim in Rome.

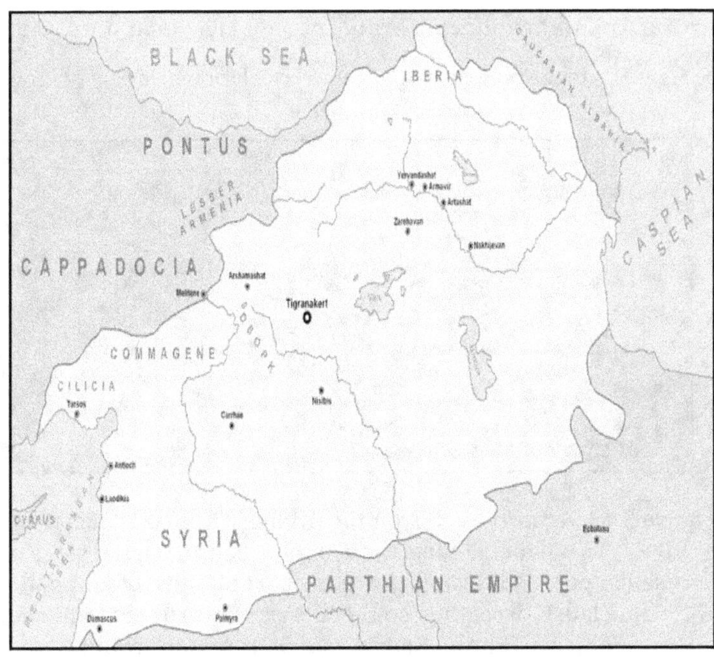

Figure 5.12. Map of the Parthian Empire and its location relative to ancient Roman province of Syria in 80 BC.
(Map courtesy of Aivazovsky,
http://en.wikipedia.org/wiki/File:Armenian_Empire.png.)

Perhaps Crassus desperately wanted to cap his career with a grand military victory and earn a triumph and parade through Rome in god-like fashion with captives and booty in tow (as depicted in figure 5.13). By this time, Pompey, Crassus' lifelong competitor for glory, had earned three triumphs, but Caesar had not yet received his, which would be a quadruple triumph for his victories on four continents. And Crassus? He would not live to see Caesar's triumph nor would he ever celebrate one of his own.

Figure 5.13. A marble relief on the Arch of Titus constructed circa AD 82. This panel depicts the Temple spoils from the siege of Jerusalem paraded through Rome as part of Titus' triumph in AD 71. Some laurel-wreathed soldiers carry placards explaining the objects. (Photo: Courtesy of Shutterstock.com.)

Jealousy of Pompey's Triumphs

Crassus might even have been present in Rome for all Pompey's magnificent victory celebrations, and it is difficult to imagine he could reflect on his accomplishments without great jealousy of Pompey's military successes and his three triumphs. A triumphant

Pompey was even commemorated on a gold coin that depicted him in his triumphal chariot with the title MAGNUS (figure 5.14). Crassus, despite his love of gold, unlikely treasured the coin of Pompey, for Plutarch informed his readers that on one occasion, when someone announced, "Pompeius the Great was approaching, Crassus smiled, and asked, 'How great was he?'" (Plutarch, *Crassus* 7).

Figure 5.14. A gold coin minted to commemorate one or all of Pompey's three triumphs (Beard 2007, 20).[11] The border surrounding the head is "in the form of a laurel wreath, one of the distinctive accessories of the general and his soldiers at a triumph" (Beard 2007, 19).[12] On the right Pompey is depicted riding in his triumphal chariot.

Additional Evidence of Crassus' Jealousy

Plutarch reported another indicator of Crassus' jealousy toward Pompey that took place at the end of their first consulship together in 70 BC. As the exiting consuls addressed the people, an equestrian told of a dream in which Jupiter commanded the man to say to the consuls that they should lay down their responsibilities as friends. Plutarch describes what next occurred:

> *Upon the man saying this, and the assembly bidding the consuls be reconciled, Pompeius stood silent; but Crassus offering his right hand first, said, "Citizens, I do not consider that I am humbling myself or doing anything unworthy of me when I make the advance towards good-will and friendship to Pompeius, to whom you gave the name of Magnus before he had a beard, and voted a triumph before he was a senator.* (Plutarch, *Crassus* 12)

On the surface, Crassus paid tribute to his younger colleague in a complimentary fashion, but let's look more closely. In this short little speech, Crassus reminded the audience that even before he shaved, Pompey received the title Magnus, (from the feared dictator Sulla), and he was granted his first triumph before he was a senator (again, allowed by Sulla even though it was against tradition). Add in Crassus' denial that he was doing anything "unworthy" by ignoring Pompey's silence or by acceding to Jupiter's command, and we see a backhanded toast to Pompey with very sharp edges.

An Alternative Theory for Crassus' Motives

F. E. Adcock, in his 1966 biography of Crassus contends that it was not just a need to rival the military glory of Pompey (and Caesar) that Crassus sought in Parthia, but also additional wealth (Parthia was thought to be an extremely wealthy empire).[13] Greed was another potential driver of the actions Crassus now undertook.

Adcock describes Crassus' desire for wealth as a hunger that "gr[ew] with eating" (Adcock 1966, 49).[14] Adcock also states that the most sought-after and rare fabric in ancient Rome was Chinese silk, which had just made its way into the hands of wealthy Romans and that, if Crassus defeated Parthia, he would not only have booty from the campaign, but also be able to control the nearby portion of the Silk Road in Northern Mesopotamia leading to Rome. With that control, Crassus could impose duties on the silk fabrics on their way to Rome and control its distribution (Adcock 1966, 49).[15]

If Crassus had done as Adcock suggests, he would have resembled the robber barons of the Middle Ages even more— those feudal lords who hindered commerce by imposing their tolls on transported goods in territories they controlled. Crassus' defeat prevented that opportunity, but Adcock's argument for avarice as a motivator is reinforced by Crassus' actions just before he began his war with the Parthians. For Crassus stopped in Rome's client kingdom of Judea, on the Mediterranean Sea, next to the province of Syria (figure 5.15).

Figure 5.15. A model of the Temple in Jerusalem as it might have looked in 54 BC. (Copyright Semenov198/Shutterstock.com.)

Crassus and the Jewish Temple

In 63 BC, nine years before Crassus' arrival in Judea, Pompey successfully (for Rome) intervened in the Kingdom of Judea, and to the Jews' horror, he and his officers entered their Temple in Jerusalem. Pompey likely saw the great wealth contained there, but removed nothing (Cicero, *Pro Flacco* 67; Smallwood 2001, 26).[16]

Crassus might have heard tales of the great amount of gold in the temple, perhaps from Pompey himself, so on his way to Parthia in 54 BC, Crassus visited the Temple himself.

Perhaps, Crassus was just looking for additional funds for his military expedition, even if it required plundering a religious sanctuary (Smallwood 2001, 36).[17] However, as we have seen, Crassus' actions reveal a darker side, and he did not depart empty-handed. Josephus, a Jewish historian writing in AD 94, reports the details of what transpired (Josephus, *Antiquities of the Jews* 14.7.1):

> *Now Crassus, as he was going upon his expedition against the Parthians, came into Judea, and carried off the money that was in the temple, which Pompey had left, being two thousand talents, and was disposed to spoil it of all the gold belonging to it, which was eight thousand talents. He also took a beam, which was made of solid beaten gold, of the weight of three* hundred *minae, each of which weighed two pounds and a half (750 pounds of gold or about 10 1/2*

talents). It was the priest who was guardian of the sacred treasures, and whose name was Eleazar, that gave him this beam, not out of a wicked design, for he was a good and a righteous man; but being entrusted with the custody of the veils belonging to the temple, which were of admirable beauty, and of very costly workmanship, and hung down from this beam, when he saw that Crassus was busy in gathering money, and was in fear for the entire ornaments of the temple, he gave him this beam of gold as a ransom for the whole, but this not till he (Crassus) had given his oath that he would remove nothing else out of the temple, but be satisfied with this only, which he should give him, being worth many ten thousand [shekels]. Now this beam was contained in a

So, we learn from Josephus (figure 5.16) that Crassus accepted a bribe from Eleazar to forgo his intended plunder, and then broke his word and pillaged the Temple of the Jews. There is no mention of what became of all the gold. This same Temple is where Jesus cast out the moneychangers and whose ruins in modern Jerusalem remain a flashpoint for the world's three major religions.

Crassus stole from the Jewish Temple what Pompey honorably left untouched. Loaded with gold and another large black mark on his reputation, Crassus marched on to fight an adversary the Roman Senate had not even declared an enemy of Rome (Plutarch, *Crassus* 16). So began the final act of Crassus' iniquitous life, which led to his ignominious death.

Figure 5.16. Roman bust thought to be the
Jewish historian Josephus who wrote
of Crassus' plunder of the Temple in Jerusalem.

Crassus' Defeat

Whether he was motivated by ambition, jealousy, or avarice, the consequences of Crassus' decision to wage war on Parthia were the same. Crassus pushed his capabilities too far with the result that the Parthian General Surenas (also known as Surena, Soren, Sorena, and Suren) (figure 5.17) with a smaller army of ten thousand defeated Crassus' forty thousand legionnaires.

Figure 5.17. A Parthian bronze, thought to be
General Surenas, in the National Museum of Iran.

A key element of victory was that Surenas modified his force
as almost exclusively mounted archers (9,000), armed with
powerful compound bows, followed by "1,000 baggage camels
laden with spare arrows" (Sampson 2008, 118–120).[18] The arrows
were barbed and, in some novel fashion, could pierce both the
Roman shields and armor (Sampson 2008, 120–121).[19] Plutarch
reported that "strange missiles preceded the appearance of the
enemy, and before one could see who sent them, they pierced
through everything that they struck" (Plutarch, *Crassus* 18.3).

Crassus' Roman legions, which had never faced a Parthian

army, were destroyed under a constant barrage of armor-piercing arrows (Sampson 2008, 123).[20] Crassus lost the war and his military standards, thirty thousand of his forty thousand soldiers, his son, and his life (Sampson 2008, 169).[21] With Crassus' death, the Republic reached the end of its life, for without Crassus on the scene, Caesar resorted to civil war to resolve his differences with Pompey and the Roman Senate.

Crassus' Death

We do not know whether Surenas ordered that molten gold be poured down Crassus' throat, for Plutarch, unlike Cassius Dio who was writing about a century later, reports only that Crassus' head and right hand were sent to Orodes II (also known as Hyrodes), the Parthian king. If the tale of the molten gold was extant in Plutarch's time, we must assume he would have retold it in his biography of Crassus, but all we have from Plutarch is silence.

Myth or not, Dio's story makes great theatre, for the Romans also believed you died as you lived; thus, Crassus would have found the death he deserved (Koster 2014, 311).[22] The ancients were not the only ones fascinated by Crassus' macabre end at his enemies' hands. Sigmund Freud, in his work *The Interpretation of Dreams* (figure 5.18), offers a strange "teachable moment" from Crassus' death.[23]

Figure 5.18. Freud's book, *The Interpretation of Dreams*, published in the US in 1900. In the book, Freud uses Crassus' desecration by the Parthians as an example of wish fulfillment.

Freud, in the sixth chapter of his famous text, offers an example of wish fulfillment that "the queen of the Parthians chose for the triumvir Crassus. Believing he had undertaken the campaign out of greed for gold, she caused molten gold to be poured into the throat of the corpse. 'Now hast thou what thou hast longed for.'" Freud picked up the cudgel passed from Cicero to Plutarch then Dio, and landed another telling blow on Crassus' legacy.

Positive Comments on Crassus

We began this text lamenting the absence of details from Crassus' businesses and the multiplicity of anecdotes of his avarice. Crassus' enemies worked hard to besmirch his reputation, with much help from the man himself, but they did not stop there. Crassus' political opponents also targeted his wife Tertulla, for it was rumored that the adulterous Caesar seduced her (Suetonius, *Caesar* 50.1; Ward 1977, 292, n. 11).[24]

In an age where men changed wives as easily as they changed their togas, Crassus remained unmoved. He likely saw the charge of wifely infidelity for what it was—an effort to attack him and weaken the Triumvirate. Crassus did not divorce his wife, nor did he abandon Caesar. So, there was loyalty in the man. In fact, Plutarch, in his biography, even pays Crassus a weak compliment or two.

Plutarch writes, "Crassus was hospitable to strangers, for his house was open to all," and "He pleased people, also, by his friendly and affable manner in taking them by the hand and addressing them; for Crassus never met a Roman, however low and humble his condition might be, without returning his salute and addressing him by his name" (Plutarch, *Crassus* 3). This behavior is hardly the behavior of an arrogant plutocrat, but unfortunately, not anywhere near an exoneration of Crassus from the long cascade of sins we have seen offered by our surviving ancient sources.

In concluding his modern biography of Crassus, Allen Ward,

too, commented on his subject's limited positive side. Ward dismisses the alleged greed as the sole driver of Crassus' life and writes, "In one arena alone could Crassus be called immoderate: this was ambition, not avarice. What many have seen as avarice and unbounded greed in Crassus is a function of his supreme ambition to be the most important man at Rome, the *princeps civitatis* (First Citizen)" (Ward 1977, 293).[25] A positive, but not much of one at that!

Crassus, the First Robber Baron

We have completed our study of Crassus' business practices, and we must now try to answer whether Crassus was the robber baron archetype. This author would argue that the scale tilts towards the affirmative. Crassus was innovative in his methods, but innovative in a way that consistently exploited the vulnerable (as did the robber barons), often pursued profit more for the love of profit than need (as did the robber barons), and occasionally (for example, his donatives to Hercules), he was publicly generous to perhaps counteract his perceived vice of greed (as did many robber barons). Crassus, in a side-by-side comparison (table 5.1), clearly did not differ greatly from the Gilded Age's robber barons, for Crassus demonstrated too many of the robber barons' exploitive practices to be anything better.

Table 5.1. Comparing Crassus' Business Practices to Those of the Robber Barons.

Exploitive Practices of the Robber Barons	Exploitive Practices of Crassus
Used political influence for personal gain	Used his political influence to further his financial needs (for example, Asian tax collectors)
Bribed judges and legislators at all government levels	Offered interest-free loans and discounted housing prices to other senators
Controlled resources	Controlled multiple tin and silver mines, but not a monopoly
Manipulated stock	Owned stock in tax-collecting companies, but no evidence of price manipulation
Paid low wages	Exploited slave workforce for profit
Conducted predatory pricing to gain a monopoly	Purchased proscribed and threatened properties under fire sale, leading to control of much of Rome's real estate market

So, for Crassus, the negatives overwhelm the few entries on the positive side of the ledger, and a comparison of the robber barons' malfeasance to that of Crassus is damning—Crassus set the bar low for future generations of robber barons. However, some recent writers have argued persuasively that despite their moral shortcomings, the robber barons of the late nineteenth and early twentieth centuries helped make America great by creating the modern corporation, "a new kind of highly productive economic organism, structurally and functionally different from the ones that had occupied the landscape previously" (Porter 2006, 28)"[26] and in key industries "pushed the United States into world leadership" (Folsom 1987, xi).[27]

In the cases of Vanderbilt with his railroads, Morgan with his bank, and Rockefeller with Standard Oil, each grew huge enterprises that lasted long after the founding robber baron departed the scene. But not so Crassus—his wealth creation engines died with him.

Now, in Crassus' defense, Rome was a pre-industrial society, so perhaps we are unfair. However, it is difficult to see how Crassus' economic activities added to the greatness of the Roman Republic. Does this limitation disqualify Crassus from being credited as a prototypical robber baron? Hardly, for if we look more deeply into the underbelly of the Gilded Age, we find a representative robber baron who resembles the Crassus model even more. That man was Wall Street financier Jay Gould.

Jay Gould

Jay Gould (figure 5.19) was born dirt poor in rural Roxbury, New York, in 1836, and though he was more than four decades younger that Cornelius Vanderbilt, Vanderbilt's biographer described him as "the most dangerous enemy of Vanderbilt's long life" (Stiles 2010, 381).[28] Vanderbilt himself said of Gould, "I consider Mr. Jay Gould a damned villain" (Stiles 2010, 530).[29] And the powerful J. P. Morgan who had "been outmaneuvered by Gould, was always torn between keeping him at wary distance and chasing after his business" (Morris 2005, 21).[30]

The diminutive Gould (he was barely five feet tall) was an early Wall Street speculator whose machinations terrorized his fellow robber barons—one said of him, "his touch is death" (Morris 2005, 21).[31] If Gould was a threat to the robber barons themselves, what did typical investors face if Gould cast his eye on their enterprises?

Even Charles R. Morgan, in his book arguing the importance of the great robber barons to expanding the American economy, admitted that with Gould, "Time and again, unsuspecting investors struggling to rescue their business or recover their funds would suddenly be confronted by the specter of

Gould, as if he had risen from the gloom, snatching away both their company and their money" (Morris 2005, 21).[32]

Figure 5.19. Jay Gould in an undated photo.

Gould was a financial genius and likely the most hated businessman of the nineteenth century (imagine Gordon Gekko in the film *Wall Street*, but unconstrained by any governmental oversight). Gould in his Wall Street career not only used stock manipulation (he was far from alone in this) to gain control of business he desired (he was fond of the railroads and telegraph companies), but also purchased the *New York World* to manipulate the news other Wall Street brokers read.

Gould even tried to corner the gold market in 1869, which triggered a panic of such proportions that President Grant was forced to release federal gold stocks to restore market confidence (Renehen 2006, 176).[33] Gould was frequently caricatured in political cartoons of the day as a large black spider capturing innocent investors and whole companies by "spinning huge webs, in corners and in the dark" (Adams & Adams 1968, 105).[34] In fact, Gould was even depicted as Satan (figure 5.20).

A recent Jay Gould biographer, who entitled his book *Dark Genius of Wall Street: The Misunderstood Life of Jay Gould, King of the Robber Barons,* admitted Gould was "guilty of every crime transacted by his generation of American capitalists" (Renehen 2006, xi).[35] We begin to think Gould had even worse press than Crassus did. And perhaps, he did.

When Gould died at 56, the *New York Times,* on December 3, 1892, wrote in its obituary, "It would be at least very difficult to show that the Nation as a whole is a dollar richer by the existence of Jay Gould." This man perhaps best epitomized all that was wrong with the Gilded Age, and here, too, we see a deep resemblance to our prototypical robber baron, Crassus, and all that was wrong with the Late Roman Republic.

Figure 5.20. Jay Gould caricatured as Satan with his minions controlling the telegraph wires and trains in Hades.

Beneath all the criticisms piled on Crassus' deeds and death lies buried a complex and flawed man, a man whose lessons in entrepreneurial thinking could only be distilled from his lifetime's accumulation of dirt with great effort. Those carefully extracted lessons, drawn, as Crassus' wealth, from exploiting the Late Roman Republic's predilection for war and vulnerability to fire, are immune to the passage of time. The ten lessons that emerged from the harsh actions of the world's first robber baron are as relevant today as they would have been in America's Gilded Age:

The Ten Business Lessons of Marcus Crassus

Lesson 1: Envisage Your Future

Lesson 2: Control Your Future

Lesson 3: Carefully Assess Risk/Reward Tradeoffs

Lesson 4: Have the Courage of Your Convictions

Lesson 5: Know Your Brief

Lesson 6: One Man's Problem Is Another's Business Opportunity

Lesson 7: Obtain the Best Talent Available

Lesson 8: Leverage Your Past

Lesson 9: Stay Committed to Your Vision

Lesson 10: A Friend in Need Is a Friend Indeed

Appendix A. Catiline Conspiracy

In a court overseen by Julius Caesar in 64 BC, a Roman aristocrat, Catiline, was acquitted of killing, nearly two decades earlier under Sulla, "a number of citizens who had been legally proscribed, and having collected the price on their heads from the public treasury" (Meier 1982, 149).[1] In 64 BC, Catiline ran for consul but lost to Cicero. Then, in late 63 BC, he was again defeated trying to gain the consulship for the year 62 BC.

Catiline's solution was to attempt an armed insurrection, murder Cicero, and seize power. Fulvia, a conspirator's mistress, warned Cicero of the conspiracy. Cicero condemned Catiline in the Senate (figure 1.2), and the Senate voted for the death penalty for the leading conspirators. (For this vote, his enemies later exiled Cicero). Caesar argued for leniency, and Crassus absented himself from the thorny debate on punishment for fellow senators.

One key program of the conspirators was the cancellation of debts, which was attractive to the poor, disaffected Sullan veterans and aristocrats who found themselves deeply in debt. We can imagine that such a program and its leader would have been anathema to Crassus—likely one of the largest debt holders in Rome. And, in fact, Crassus (with other senators) turned over to

Cicero anonymous letters warning selected senators (such as Crassus) to leave the city of Rome to avoid the slaughter awaiting Catiline's enemies if he was successful in his putsch.

Ancient sources, including Plutarch, Suetonius, and Sallust (a contemporary of Crassus) all show varying amounts of early support by Crassus and Caesar for Catiline, perhaps to counterbalance Pompey's military strength (Sallust, *The War with Catiline* 17.7). However, as events evolved, Crassus and Caesar seemed to develop concern over Catiline's plan to instigate a Sulla-like civil war, and they withdrew their support (if it was ever given).

One follower of Catiline accused Crassus of involvement, but Crassus was heard to say by Sallust himself that the allegation was false and created by Cicero for political reasons (Sallust, *The War with Catiline* 48.9). Neither Cicero nor his senatorial allies (many in Crassus' debt) formally accused Crassus of any attempt to foment rebellion; however, as we have seen with many incidents involving Crassus, the details of Crassus' actions and motivations in this sordid event are sketchy, and the sense of Crassus' behind-the-scene role again seems unsavory and self-serving.

Appendix B. The Manumission of Roman Slaves

For the state to collect the 5 percent manumission tax (1/20 of the slave's value) on the freeing of a slave, one of three methods was needed to legally free the slave. The freed slave, called a *freedman*, gained significant legal rights (for example, could vote, marry, conduct business), but not all the rights of a freeborn citizen (for example, could not become a legionnaire, a magistrate, or a senator), although any child of the freed slave born after manumission was considered a full freeborn Roman citizen. The following three methods were used to formally free a slave (Massey & Mooreland 2001, 67–69):[1]

1. By census

   When a census was conducted, about every five years, but there were significant periods without electing censors and a census because of war, economic upheaval, disease, and politics. If there was a census, a slave owner merely entered the name of the slave he wished to free on the list of citizens. With the end of the Republic, this method of manumitting a slave ended, because under the emperors, there were no more censors chosen, although the conduct of a regular census continued.

2. By will

    A slave owner could free his slave or slaves in his will. This frequently used method rewarded the slave(s) for their service to the master.

3. By rod

    In this legal ceremony, conducted in the presence of a Roman magistrate, the official "touched the slave with a rod and declared that he was free and was no longer the property of the master. The master then turned the slave around and slapped him, and from that moment the slave was a free man" (Massey & Mooreland 2001, 67–69). The rationale for the slap was unclear, but it seems to have been a final insult to the slave or an initial reminder of the newly freed man's inferior status to a full citizen.

By the end of the Roman Republic, manumission became so frequent that in the early Empire under Augustus, legislation limited both the number of slaves freed in a will and the age of manumission if the owner was still alive.

Appendix C. Description of Roman Slavery (Mills)

We learned from Plutarch that Crassus "superintended" his many specialized slaves in Rome. However, Plutarch also informed us that Crassus owned great revenue-producing country estates without telling his readers how Crassus tended the much less skilled slaves involved in physical work on those farms. However, we have a graphic description of slaves working in a flourmill, perhaps not unlike one on an estate of Crassus. This description is from the mid-second century AD, nearly two centuries after Crassus' death. Although taken from a work of fiction, the hellish scene was likely drawn from personal observation, for the author traveled widely around the Roman Empire before he died (c. AD 180. Here is his depiction of the suffering of the slaves grinding flour (Apuleius, *The Golden Ass* 143–4):

> *O good Lord, what a sort of poor slaves were there; some had their skin bruised all over black and blue, some had their backs striped with lashes and were but covered rather than clothed with torn rags, some had their members only*

hidden by a narrow cloth, all wore such ragged clouts that you might perceive through them all their naked bodies, some were marked and burned in the forehead with hot irons, some had their hair half clipped, some had shackles on their legs, ugly and evil-favored, some could scarce see, their eyes and faces were so black and dim with smoke, their eyelids all cankered with the darkness of that reeking place, half-blind and sprinkled black and white with dirty flour-like boxers which fight together befouled with sand.

Appendix D. Description of Roman Slavery (Estates)

The ancient historian Cassius Dio (c. AD 155 AD–AD 235) told a story intended to show the virtue of the Emperor Augustus and the cruelty of a wealthy equestrian by the name Vedius Pollio. He revealed the life and death power slave owners held over their slaves. Dio wrote of Pollio (Dio, *Roman History* 54.23):

> *He was without any achievement of consequence in his record, but he had become exceedingly renowned for his wealth and his cruelty, so that he has even won a place in history. Most of the things that he did, it would be wearisome to relate, but I may mention that he kept in tanks huge eels trained to eat men, and was accustomed to throw to them the slaves that he desired to put to death. Once, when he was entertaining Augustus, the cupbearer shattered a crystal goblet, and without respect to the guest, he ordered that the fellow be thrown to*

> *the eels. Hereupon, the boy fell on his knees supplicating Augustus, who at first tried to persuade Pollio not to carry out his intentions. As his host would not yield the point, the Emperor said, "Bring all the rest of the drinking vessels which are of the same sort or any others of value that you may possess, for I want to use them," and when they were brought, he ordered them to be broken. The master seeing this was of course vexed, but could no longer be angry over one cup, considering the great number of others that were ruined, and could not punish his servant for what Augustus had done; therefore, reluctantly, he took no action.*

Not all slave owners were as cruel as Pollio was, and there are positive accounts in the record. As an example, I offer one from Pliny the Younger's letters (*Pliny Letters*, VIII.16):

*The sickness lately in my family, which
has carried off several of my servants,
some of them, too, in the prime of their
years, has been a great affliction to me.
I have two consolations, however,
which, though by no means equivalent
to such a grief, still are consolations.
One is, that as I have always readily
manumitted my slaves, their death does
not seem altogether immature, if they
lived long enough to receive their
freedom: the other, that I have allowed
them to make a kind of will, which I
observe as religiously as if they were
legally entitled to that privilege. I
receive and obey their last requests and
injunctions as so many authoritative
commands, suffering them to dispose of
their effects to whom they please; with
this single restriction, that they leave
them to someone in my household, for
to slaves, the house they are in is a kind*

*of state and commonwealth, so to
speak.*

Appendix E. Description of Roman Slavery (Mines)

We learned from Plutarch that Crassus owned several mines. The working conditions in the mines were brutal, and the treatment of the slaves who worked them even worse. The slaves, usually prisoners of war and convicts, were condemned to live and die in the mines, as we learn from the Greek historian Diodorus Siculus. His major surviving work, the *Historical Library*, was written during the Late Republic (60 BC–30 BC). Siculus (V.38.1) describes the hellish mines of Iberia—the Roman province in which Crassus and his family owned mines:

> But to continue with the mines, the slaves who are engaged in the working of them produce for their masters revenues in sums defying belief, but they themselves wear out their bodies both by day and by night in the diggings under the earth, dying in large numbers because of the exceptional hardships they endure. For no respite or pause is granted them in their

labors, but compelled beneath blows of the overseers to endure the severity of their plight, they throw away their lives in this wretched manner, although certain of them who can endure it, by virtue of their bodily strength and their persevering souls, suffer such hardships over a long period; indeed, death in their eyes is more to be desired than life, because of the magnitude of the hardships they must bear.

Appendix F. Description of a Roman Triumph

This description is from Plutarch's *Life of Aemilius* (sections 32–34). Lucius Aemilius Paullus Macedonicus, a two-time consul, was awarded the triumph for his defeat of Macedon in 168 BC (figure F.1). Aemilius died in 160 BC, a little more than a century before the death of Crassus:

> *It is said to have been celebrated thus. The people, dressed in white robes, looked on from platforms erected in the horse course, which they call the Circus, and round the Forum, and in all other places, which gave them a view of the procession. Every temple was open and full of flowers and incense, and many officials with staves drove off people who formed disorderly mobs and kept the way clear. The procession was divided into three days. The first scarcely sufficed for the display of the captured statues, sculptures, and*

paintings, which were carried on two hundred and fifty carriages.

On the following day, the finest and most costly of the Macedonian arms and armor were borne along in many wagons, glittering with newly burnished brass and iron and arranged in a carefully studied disorder, helmets upon shields, and corslets upon greaves, with Cretan targets, Thracian wicker shields and quivers mixed with horses' bits, naked swords rising out of these, and the long spears of the phalanx ranged in order above them, making a harmonious clash of arms, as they were arranged to clatter when they were driven along, with a harsh and menacing sound so that the sight of them even after victory was not without terror. After the wagons which bore the arms walked three thousand men, carrying the silver coin in seven hundred and fifty earthen vessels, each carrying three talents, and borne by four men. Others carried the silver drinking horns and goblets and chalices, each of them disposed so that it could be well seen, and all remarkable for their size and the boldness of their carving.

On the third day, at earliest dawn, marched the trumpeters, not playing the music of a march, but sounding the notes, which animate the Romans for a charge. After them were led along a hundred and twenty fat oxen with gilded horns, adorned with crowns and wreaths. They were led by youths clad in finely fringed waistcloths in which to do the sacrifice, while boys carried the wine for the libations in gold and silver vessels. After these came men carrying the gold coin, divided into vessels of three talents each like the silver. The number of these vessels was eighty all but three. Then came those who carried

the consecrated bowl, which Aemilius
had made of ten talents of gold
adorned with jewels, and men carrying
the plate of Antigonus and Seleukus
and cups of Therikles-ware and all
Perseus's own service of gold plate.

Next came the chariot of Perseus
with his armor; and his crown set upon
the top of his armor: and then after a
little interval came the captive children
of the king and with them a tearful
band of nurses and teachers, who held
out their hands in supplication to the
spectators, and taught the children to
beg them for mercy. There were two
boys and one girl, all too young to
comprehend the extent of their
misfortune. This carelessness made
their fallen state all the more pitiable
so that Perseus himself walked almost
unnoticed; for the Romans in their pity
had eyes only for the children, and
many shed tears, while all felt that the

sight was more painful than pleasing
till the children were gone by.

Behind the children and their
attendants walked Perseus himself,
dressed in a dark-colored cloak with
country boots, seeming to be dazed and
stupefied by the greatness of his fall. A
band of his friends and associates
followed him with grief-laden
countenances, and by their constantly
looking at Perseus and weeping, gave
the spectators the idea that they
bewailed his fate without taking any
thought about their own. However,
Perseus had sent to Aemilius asking to
be excused the walking in procession;
but he, as it seems in mockery of his
cowardice and love of life, answered,
"That was formerly in his own hands,
and is now if he pleases." Meaning that
death was preferable to dishonor; but
the dastard had not spirit enough for

that, but buoyed up by some hope, became a part of his own spoils.

After these were borne golden crowns, four hundred in number, which the cities of Greece had sent to Aemilius with deputations, in recognition of his success. Next, he came himself, sitting in a splendid chariot, a man worth looking upon even without his present grandeur, dressed in a purple robe sprinkled with gold, and holding a branch of laurel in his right hand. All the army was crowned with laurel and followed the car of the general in military array, at one time singing and laughing over old country songs, then raising in chorus the paean of victory and recital of their deeds, to the glory of Aemilius, who was gazed upon and envied by all, disliked by no good man.

Figure F.1: Painting of *The Triumph of Aemilius,* created in 1789 by the French painter Carle Vernet.

Notes

Introduction

1. Michael Grant, *The Ancient Historians* (New York: Barnes and Noble, Inc., 1970), 310.

2. Allen Mason Ward, *Marcus Crassus and the Late Roman Republic* (Columbia: University of Missouri Press, 1977).

3. Henry Mintzberg, Bruce Ahlstrand, and Joseph Lampel, *Strategy Safari: A Guided Tour Through The Wilds* of *Strategic Management* (New York: Free Press, 2005), 123–147.

4. Tom Holland, *Rubicon: The Last Years of the Roman Republic* (New York: Anchor Press, 2003), 136.

5. Robert C. Lerner, *Entrepreneurship and Ethics in Ancient Rome: The Management Lessons of Pliny the Younger* (Oshawa, CA: Multi-Media Publications, 2013).

6. Robert C. Lerner, *Career Turbulence: Ancient Lessons for Survival in the Modern Workplace* (Oshawa, CA: Multi-Media Publications, 2014).

7. Ward, *Marcus Crassus*; B. A. Marshall, *Crassus: A Political Biography* (Amsterdam: Adolf M. Hakkert, 1976).

8. F. E. Adcock, *Marcus Crassus, Millionaire* (Cambridge: W. Hefner & Sons, LTD, 1966).

9. Ron Chernow, *The House of Morgan: An American Banking Dynasty and the Rise of Modern Finance* (New York: Grove Press, 2010).

10. JPMorgan Chase & Co., "About Us," *JPMorgan Chase*, 2018, https://www.jpmorganchase.com/corporate/About-JPMC/about-us.

11. *New York Times*, "The Wealthiest Americans Ever," July 15, 2007, http://www.nytimes.com/ref/business/20070715_GILDED_GRAPHIC.html#.

12. Ibid.

13. T. J. Stiles, *The First Tycoon: The Epic Life of Cornelius Vanderbilt* (New York: Vintage Books, 2010), 116.

14. Mintzberg, Ahlstrand, and Lampel, *Strategy Safari*, 123–147.

Chapter 1

1. Ward, *Marcus Crassus*; Marshall, *Crassus*, 74.

2. Arthur Keaveney, *Sulla: The Last Republican* (New York: Routledge, 2005), 109.

3. Ward, *Marcus Crassus*; Marshall, *Crassus*, 61.

4. American Marketing Association, "Dictionary," https://www.ama.org/resources/pages/dictionary.aspx?dLetter=V.

5.   Amar Bhide, "How Entrepreneurs Craft Strategies That Work," *Harvard Business Review* 72, no. 2 (March-April 1994): 150–161.

6.   Ibid., p. 152.

7.   Julian E. Lange and others, "Pre-start-up Formal Business Plans and Post-start-up Performance: A Study of 116 New Ventures," *Venture Capital* 9, no. 4 (October 2007): 237–256.

8.   Ward, *Marcus Crassus*, 49.

9.   Ibid., 69, n40.

10. Ibid., 61.

11. Robin Seager, *Pompey the Great* (Malden: Blackwell Publishing, 2002), 21–23.

12. Ibid., 26.

13. Ibid.

14. Stiles, *The First Tycoon,* 434.

15. Ibid.

Chapter 2

1.   Anthony Everitt, *Cicero: The Life and Times of Rome's Greatest Politician* (New York: Random House, 2003) 41.

2.   Geoffrey Perret, *Lincoln's War: The Untold Story of America's Greatest President as Commander in Chief* (New York: Random House, 2004), 403; Carl Sandburg, *Abraham Lincoln: The War*

Years, vol. 4 (New York: Harcourt, Brace & World, Inc., 1939), 227.

3. Perret, *Lincoln's War*, 404.

4. Ida M. Tarbell, *The Early Life of Abraham Lincoln* (S. S. McClure, Ltd., 1896; reis., Forgotten Books, 2012), 71.

5. Ward, *Marcus Crassus*, 66.

6. Adcock, *Marcus Crassus*.

7. Ward, *Marcus Crassus*, 48, n11.

8. Keaveney, *Sulla*, 145.

9. Ibid.

10. Everitt, Cicero, 115.

11. Ward, *Marcus Crassus*, 66.

12. Ibid.

13. Marshall, *Crassus*, 183.

14. Keaveney, *Sulla*, 126.

Chapter 3

1. John E. Stambaugh, *The Ancient Roman City (Ancient Society and History)* (Baltimore: The Johns Hopkins University Press, 1988), 89.

2.   H. V. Canter, "Conflagrations in Ancient Rome," *The Classical Journal* 27, no. 4 (January 1931): 286.

3. Stambaugh, *The Ancient Roman City*, 90; 338, n6.

4. RomanEmpire.net, "Marcus Licinius Crassus (d. 53 BC)," *Illustrated History of the Roman Empire*, http://www.roman-empire.net/republic/crassus-index.html.

5. Joshua J. Mark, "Ancient Rome," *Ancient History™ Encyclopedia*, September 2, 2009, http://www.ancient.eu.com/Rome/.

6. Reynolds, P. K. Baillie, *The Vigiles of Imperial Rome* (Chicago: Ares Publishers, Inc., 1996), 20–21.

7. Ibid., 22–25.

8. Canter, "Conflagrations," 287–8.

9. Ibid., 287.

10. Reynolds, *The Vigiles*, 14.

11. Canter, "Conflagrations," 288.

12. Reynolds, *The Vigiles*, 94.

13. Ward, *Marcus Crassus*, 73.

14. *Wikipedia*, "History of Firefighting," http://en.wikipedia.org/wiki/History_of_firefighting.

15. Reynolds, *The Vigiles*, 83.

16. Ibid., 83, 94, 97.

17. NYC Council, *Report on the Fiscal Year 2015 Executive Budget for the Fire Department, June 2, 2014*, 4.

18. Bhide, "How Entrepreneurs Craft Strategies That Work," 151.

19. Ward, *Marcus Crassus*, 73.

20. Ibid.

21. Ward, *Marcus Crassus*, 73–74.

22. Alice Hill Byrne, *Titus Pomponius Atticus: Chapters of a Biography* (Charleston: BiblioLife, LLC., 1920), 15.

23. Ibid., 14.

24. Matthew Josephson, *The Robber Barons* (San Diego: Harcourt, Inc., 1995), 61.

Chapter 4

1. Lerner, *Career Turbulence.*

2. Stambaugh, *The Ancient Roman City*, 42–43.

3. E. Badian, *Publicans and Sinners: Private Enterprise in the Service of the Roman Republic* (Ithaca: Cornell University Press, 1983) 63.

4. Ibid., 103.

5. Stiles, *The First Tycoon*, 223.

Chapter 5

1. Ward, *Marcus Crassus*, 75, n57.

2. T. J. Cadoux, "Catiline and the Vestal Virgins," *Historia: Zeitschrift für Alte Geschichte* 54, no. 2 (2005): 165, http://www.jstor.org/stable/443676.

3. Ward, *Marcus Crassus*, 74–75.

4. Melissa S. Cardon, Richard Sudek, and Cheryl Mitteness, "The Impact of Perceived Entrepreneurial

Passion on Angel Investing," *Frontiers of Entrepreneurship Research* 29, no. 2 (2009), http://digitalknowledge.babson.edu/fer/vol29/iss2/1.

5. Ibid., 6.

6. Daniel Isenberg, "The Danger of Entrepreneurial Passion," *HBR Blog Network* (January 6, 2010), http://blogs.hbr.org/2010/01/the-danger-of-entrepreneurial/.

7. Barry Strauss, *The Spartacus War* (New York: Simon and Schuster, 2009).

8. Sandra R. Joshel, *Slavery in the Roman World* (New York: Cambridge University Press, 2010).

9. Seager, *Pompey the Great*, 36.

10. Christian Meier, *Caesar: A Biography* (London: Harper Collins Publishers, 1982), 130.

11. Mary Beard, *The Roman Triumph* (Cambridge: The Belknap Press of Harvard University, 2007), 20.

12. Ibid., 19.

13. Adcock, *Marcus Crassus*.

14. Ibid., 49.

15. Ibid.

16. E. Mary Smallwood, *The Jews under Roman Rule: From Pompey to Diocletian: A Study in Political Relations (Boston: Brill Academic Publishers, Inc., 2001), 26.*

17. Ibid., 36.

18. Gareth C. Sampson, *The Defeat of Rome in the East: Crassus, The Parthians, and the Disastrous Battle of Carrhae, 53 BC* (Drexel Hill: Casemate, 2008), 118–120.

19. Ibid., 120–121.

20. Ibid., 123.

21. Ibid., 169.

22. Isabel K. Koster, "How to Kill a Villain: The Deaths of Quintus Pleminius," *The Classical Journal* 109, no. 3 (Feb.–Mar. 2014): 311.

23. Sigmund Freud, *The Interpretation of Dreams,* 3rd ed., trans. A. A. Brill (New York: The Macmillan Company, 1913; Bartleby.com, 2010), www.bartleby.com/285/. .

24. Ward, *Marcus Crassus*, 292, n11.

25. Ibid., 293.

26. Glenn Porter, *The Rise of Big Business 1860–1920* (Malden: Wiley-Blackwell, 2006), 28.

27. Burton W. Folsom Jr., *Entrepreneurs vs. the State: A New Look at the Rise of Big Business in America, 1840–1920* (Reston: Young America's Foundation, 1987), xi.

28. Stiles, *The First Tycoon*, 381.

29. Ibid., 530.

30. Charles R. Morris, *The Tycoons: How Andrew Carnegie, John D. Rockefeller, Jay Gould and J. P. Morgan Invented the American Super Economy* (New York: Times Books/Henry Holt and Company, 2005).

31. Ibid., 21.

32. Ibid.

33. Edward J. Renehan Jr., *Dark Genius of Wall Street: The Misunderstood Life of Jay Gould, King of the Robber Barons* (New York: Basic Books, 2006), 176.

34. Charles Francis Adams Jr. and Henry Adams, *Chapters of Erie* (Ithaca: Cornell University Press, 1968), 105.

35. Renehan, *Dark Genius of Wall Street*, xi.

Appendix A

1.   Meier, *Caesar*, 149.

Appendix B

1.   Michael Massey and Paul Mooreland, *Slavery in Ancient Rome* (London: Bristol Classical Press, 2001), 67–69.

2.   Ibid.

Bibliography

Ancient Sources

Apuleius, Lucius. *The Golden Ass*. Translated by William Adlington. Hertfordshire: Wadsworth Editions Limited, 1996.

Caesar. *The Civil War*. Translated by Jane P. Gardner. New York: Penguin Books, 1976.

Cicero. *Defense Speeches*. Translated by D. H. Berry. Oxford: Oxford University Press, 2000.

Cicero. *Letters to Atticus*. Translated by D. R. Shackleton Bailey. Vols. I–IV. Cambridge: Harvard University Press, 1999.

Cicero. *Letters to Friends*. Translated by D.R. Shackleton Bailey. Vol. I. Cambridge: Harvard University Press, 2001.

Cicero. *Letters to Quintus and Brutus*. Translated by D. R. Shackleton Bailey. Cambridge: Harvard University Press, 2002.

Cicero. *On Duties*. Translated by Walter Miller. Cambridge: Harvard University Press, 2005.

Cicero. *Pro Flacco*. Translated by C. Macdonald. Cambridge: Harvard University Press, 1996.

Dio, Cassius. *Roman History*. Translated by Earnest Cary. Vols. III–VII. Cambridge: Harvard University Press, 2005.

Horace. *Satires and Epistles*. Translated by Niall Rudd. London: Penguin Books, 1979.

Josephus. *Antiquities* of *the Jews*. Translated by William Whiston. Grand Rapids: Kregel Publications, 1995.

Maximus, Valerius. *Memorable* Doings *and Sayings*. Translated by D. R. Shackleton Bailey. Vol. II. Cambridge: Harvard University Press, 2000.

Nepos, Cornelius. *Latin Historians*. Translated by John C. Rolfe. Cambridge: Harvard University Press, 2005.

Pliny the Elder. *Natural History Books*. Vols. XXXIII–XXXV. Translated by H. Rackham. Cambridge: Harvard University Press, 1999.

Pliny the Younger. *Pliny Letters and Panegyricus*. Vols. I and II. Cambridge: Harvard University Press, 1969.

Plutarch. *Lives*. Translated by Aubrey Stewart and George Long. London: George Bell & Sons, 1894. *Project Gutenberg*. http://www.gutenberg.org/files/14033/14033-h/14033-h.htm.

Sallust. *The War with Catiline*. Translated by J. C. Rolfe, Revised by John T. Ramsey. Cambridge: Harvard University Press, 2013.

Siculus, Diodorus. *Library* of *History*. Translated by C. H. Oldfather. Books IV.59–VIII. Cambridge: Harvard University Press, 1939.

Suetonius. *The Twelve Caesars*. Translated by John C. Rolfe. Vol.
I. Cambridge: Harvard University Press, 2001.

Secondary Sources

Adams Jr., Charles Francis, and Henry Adams. *Chapters of Erie*.
        Ithaca: Cornell University Press, 1968.

Adcock, F. E. *Marcus Crassus, Millionaire*. Cambridge: W. Hefner &
        Sons, LTD., 1966.

Andreau, Jean. *Banking and Business in the Roman World*. Cambridge:
Cambridge University

    Press, 1999.

Badian, E. *Publicans and Sinners: Private Enterprise in the Service of the
        Roman Republic*. Ithaca: Cornell University Press, 1983.

Beard, Mary. *The Roman Triumph*. Cambridge: The Belknap Press of
        Harvard University, 2007.

Bhide, Amar. "How Entrepreneurs Craft Strategies That Work."
        Harvard Business Review 72, no. 2 (March-April 1994).

Bird, Barbara. "The Roman God Mercury: An Entrepreneurial
        Archetype." *Journal* of *Management Inquiry* 1, no. 3 (Sept.1,
        1992).

http://jmi.sagepub.com/content/1/3/205.

Byrne, Alice Hill. *Titus Pomponius Atticus: Chapters of a Biography*.
Charleston: BiblioLife, LLC., 1920.

Cadoux, T. J. "Catiline and the Vestal Virgins. *Historia: Zeitschrift für
Alte Geschichte* 54, no. 2 (2005).
http://www.jstor.org/stable/443676.

—. *Marcus Crassus: A Revaluation (Greece & Rome)*. 2nd Series. Vol. 3.
No. 2. Cambridge: Cambridge
University Press, 1956. http://www.jstor.org/stable/641367.

Canter, H. V. "Conflagrations in Ancient Rome." *The Classical
Journal* 27, no. 4 (January 1931).

Cardon, Melissa S., Richard Sudek, and Cheryl Mitteness. "The
Impact of Perceived Entrepreneurial Passion on Angel
Investing." *Frontiers of Entrepreneurship Research* 29, no. 2
(2009).

Chernow, Ron. *The House of Morgan: An American Banking Dynasty
and the Rise of Modern Finance* . New York: Grove Press,
2010.

—. *Titan: The Life of John D. Rockefeller*. New York: Vintage Books,
2004.

Collins, Orvis, and David G. Moore. *The Organization Makers: A
Behavioral Study of Independent Entrepreneurs*. New York:
Appleton-Century-Crofts, 1970.

Deutsch, Monroe E. "Pompey's Three Triumphs." *Classical Philology*

19, no. 3 (Mar. 1924).

"Dictionary." *American Marketing Association.*
https://www.ama.org/resources/pages/dictionary.aspx?d
Letter=V.

Everitt, Anthony. *Cicero: The Life and Times of Rome's Greatest
Politician.* New York: Random House, 2003.

Folsom Jr., Burton W. *Entrepreneurs vs. the State: A New Look at the
Rise of Big Business in America, 1840–1920.* Reston: Young
America's Foundation, 1987.

Freud, Sigmund. *The Interpretation of Dreams.* 3rd. Translated by A.
A. Brill. New York: Bartleby.com, 2010.

Goodman, Rob and Jimmy Soni. *Rome's Last Citizen: The Life and
Legacy* of *Cato, Mortal Enemy* of *Caesar.*
New York: Thomas Dunne Books, 2012.

Goodwin, Doris Kearns. *The Bully Pulpit: Theodore Roosevelt, William
Taft and the Golden Age of
Journalism.* New York: Simon Shuster, 2013.

Grant, Michael. *The Ancient Historians.* New York: Barnes and
Noble, Inc., 1970.

Gruen, Erich S. *The Last Generation* of *the Roman Republic.* Berkeley:
University of California Press, 1995.

Hingley, Richard. *Globalizing Roman Culture: Unity, Diversity and
Empire.* New York: Routledge, 2010.

"History of Firefighting." *Wikipedia*. n.d.
http://en.wikipedia.org/wiki/History_of_firefighting.

Holland, Tom. *Rubicon: The Last Years of the Roman Republic*. New York: Anchor Press, 2003.

Isaacson, Walter. *Steve Jobs*. New York: Simon & Schuster, 2011.

Isenberg, Daniel. *The Danger of Entrepreneurial Passion*. January 6, 2010. http://blogs.hbr.org/2010/01/the-danger-of-entrepreneurial/.

Jobs, Steve. "2005 Commencement Address to the Graduating Students of Stanford University."
http://news.stanford.edu/news/2005/june15.

Jones, David. *The Bankers of Puteoli: Finance, Trade and Industry in the Roman World*. Gloucestershire: Tempus Publishing Limited, 2006.

Josephson, Matthew. *The Robber Barons*. San Diego: Harcourt, Inc., 1995.

Joshel, Sandra R. *Slavery in the Roman World*. New York: Cambridge University Press, 2010.

JPMorgan Chase & Co. *About Us*. 2018.
https://www.jpmorganchase.com/corporate/About-JPMC/about-us.

Keaveney, Arthur. *Sulla: The Last Republican*. New York: Routledge, 2005.

Klein, Maury. *The Life and Legend of Jay Gould*. Baltimore: The Johns Hopkins University Press, 1986.

Koster, Isabel K. "How to Kill a Villain: The Deaths of Quintus Pleminius." *The Classical Journal* 109, no. 3 (Feb–Mar 2014).

Lange, Julian E., Aleksandar Mollow, Michael Pearlmutter, Sunil Singh, and William D. Bygrave. "Pre-start-up Formal Business Plans and Post-start-up Performance: A Study of 116 New Ventures." *Venture Capital* 9, no. 4 (October 2007).

Lerner, Robert C. *Career Turbulence: Ancient Lessons for Survival in the Modern Workplace*. Oshawa: Multi-Media Publications, 2014.

—. *Customer Acquisition Strategies: Modern Lessons from Ancient Rome's Greatest Entrepreneurs*. Oshawa: Multi-Media Publications, 2016.

—. *Entrepreneurship and Ethics in Ancient Rome: The Management Lessons of Pliny the Younger*. Oshawa: Multi-Media Publications, 2013.

Mark, Joshua J. "Ancient Rome." *Ancient History*™ *Encyclopedia*. September 2, 2009. http://www.ancient.eu.com/Rome/.

Marshall, B. A. *Crassus: A Political Biography*. Amsterdam: Adolf M. Hakkert, 1976.

Marzano, Annalisa. "Hercules and the Triumphal Feast for the

Roman People." *Transforming Historical*

Landscapes in the Ancient Empires.* British Archeological Reports,
International Series.

Oxford: John and Erica Hedges Ltd., 1986.

Massey, Michael, and Paul Mooreland. *Slavery in Ancient Rome.*
London: Bristol Classical Press, 2001.

Meier, Christian. *Caesar: A Biography.* London: Harper-Collins
Publishers, 1982.

Millar, Fergus. *The Crowd in Rome in the Late Republic.* Ann Arbor:
The University of Michigan Press, 1998.

Mintzberg, Henry, Bruce Ahlstrand, and Joseph Lampel. *Strategy
Safari: A Guided Tour Through The Wilds of Strategic
Management.* New York: Free Press, 2005.

Morris, Charles R. *The Tycoons: How Andrew Carnegie, John D.
Rockefeller, Jay Gould and J. P. Morgan Invented the American
Super Economy.* New York: Times Books/Henry Holt and
Company, 2005.

Mullins, John W., and David Forlani. *Differences in Perception and
Behavior: A Comparative Study of New Ventures Decisions of
Managers and Entrepreneurs.* Delivered at the 1998 Babson
College Entrepreneurship Research Conference.

New American Bible. Wichita: Fireside Bible Publishers, 1981.

New York Times. "The Wealthiest Americans Ever." July 15, 2007.
http://www.nytimes.com/ref/business/20070715_GILD
ED_GRAPHIC.html#.

NYC Council. *Report on the Fiscal Year 2015 Executive Budget for the
Fire Department, June 2, 2014.*

Osgood, Josiah. *Caesar's Legacy: Civil War and the Emergence of the
Roman Empire.* New York: Cambridge University Press,
2006.

Perret, Geoffrey. *Lincoln's War: The Untold Story of America's Greatest
President as Commander in Chief.* New York: Random House,
2004.

Porter, Glenn. *The Rise of Big Business 1860-1920.* Malden: Wiley-
Blackwell, 2006.

Rawson, Elizabeth. *Cicero: A Portrait.* London: Bristol Classical
Paperbacks, 2009.

Renehan Jr., Edward J. *Dark Genius of Wall Street: The Misunderstood
Life of Jay Gould, King of the Robber Barons.* New York: Basic
Books, 2006.

Reynolds, P. K. Baillie. *The Vigiles of Imperial Rome.* Chicago: Ares
Publishers, Inc., 1996.

RomanEmpire.net. "Marcus Licinius Crassus (d. 53 BC)." *Illustrated
History of the Roman Empire.* http://www.roman-
empire.net/republic/crassus-index.html.

Sampson, Gareth C. *The Defeat of Rome in the East: Crassus, the Parthians, and the Disastrous Battle of Carrhae, 53 BC.* Drexel Hill: Casemate, 2008.

Sandburg, Carl. *Abraham Lincoln: The War Years.* Vol. 4. New York: Harcourt, Brace & World, Inc., 1939.

Seager, Robin. *Pompey the Great.* Malden: Blackwell Publishing, 2002.

Smallwood, E. Mary. *The Jews under Roman Rule: From Pompey to Diocletian: A Study in Political Relations.* Boston: Brill Academic Publishers, Inc., 2001.

Stambaugh, John E. *The Ancient Roman City (Ancient Society and History).* Baltimore: The Johns Hopkins University Press, 1988.

Stiles, T. J. *The First Tycoon: The Epic Life of Cornelius Vanderbilt.* New York: Vintage Books, 2010.

Strauss, Barry. *The Spartacus War.* New York: Simon and Schuster, 2009.

Syme, Ronald. *The Roman Revolution.* New York: Oxford University Press, 1960.

Tarbell, Ida M. *The Early Life of Abraham Lincoln* . Forgotten Books, 2012. Originally published in 1896 by S.S. McClure, Ltd.

Taylor, Lily Ross. *Party Politics in the Age of Caesar*. Berkley:

   University of California Press, 1961. Originally published

   as Volume 22 of the Sather Classical Lectures.

Tempest, Kathryn. *Cicero: Politics and Persuasion in Ancient Rome*.

London: Continuum International

   Publishing Group, 2001.

Ward, Allen Mason. *Marcus Crassus and the Late Roman Republic*.

   Columbia: University of Missouri Press, 1977.

Index of Ancient Names

Pliny the Younger 20, 77, 107, 113-115, 137, 204
Plotinus 156
Plutarch 15, 16, 18, 21, 41, 42, 45, 46-48, 53-55, 58, 60, 62-67,
  74, 78, 80, 81, 83-90, 95, 100-102, 105, 107, 108, 111, 112,
  115, 118, 120, 124, 126, 127, 134, 135, 138, 141, 142, 145,
  152, 153, 156, 158, 160, 168, 170, 177, 178, 185, 186-188, 198,
  201, 207, 209
Pompey 29-34, 54-56, 80, 85, 90, 136, 138-140, 142, 156,
  162-168, 170, 171, 173, 176-181, 186, 198
Roscius Amerinus 30
Seutonius 142, 198
Spartacus 11, 13, 14, 15, 30, 31, 34, 118, 119, 158-165, 168, 169
Sulla 30, 34, 41, 42, 47, 48, 53-56, 58-60, 62-64, 66-69, 74, 79,
  80, 86, 89. 90, 136, 162, 164, 168, 179
Surenas 184-186
Tertulla 34, 42, 65, 188
Titus 176
Trajan 107, 113, 115
Vedius Pollio 203, 204
Vibius Pacianus 43, 44

Index of Robber Barons

ABOUT THE AUTHOR

Robert Lerner is a retired business executive whose career spanned more than 30 years in the computer technology industry and culminated as President and CEO of QualxServ (now Worldwide TechServices), a multinational computer services company. In addition to *The Entrepreneurial Thinking of Marcus Crassus,* Lerner has published three other works of non-fiction that interweave ancient Roman business practices with the modern workplace - *Entrepreneurship and Ethics in Ancient Rome: The Management Lessons of Pliny the Younger, Career Turbulence: Ancient Lessons for Survival in the Modern Workplace and Customer Acquisition Strategies: Modern Lessons from Ancient Rome's Greatest Entrepreneurs.* He has also authored three works of contemporary fiction, *An Accidental Prophet, The Cinderella Vessel* and *Dog Park Diaries.*

www.ingramcontent.com/pod-product-compliance
Lightning Source LLC
Chambersburg PA
CBHW071405150726
48000CB00001B/173